THE MENTOR

ILLUMINATING THE ART OF WRITING

Emily Cunningham

The Mentor

With our thanks to Carl Styants, Editor, Writers' Forum magazine for permission to reprint these articles.

Published by Limelight Books
An imprint of The Write Factor
www.thewritefactor.co.uk

LIMELIGHT
BOOKS
A FOCUS ON NEW WRITING

The Mentor

Illuminating the Art of Writing

Contents

WHO NEEDS A MENTOR ANYWAY?

"When you're writing, do you ever feel like you need a therapist, friend, teacher or reviewer – or perhaps all of these rolled into one – to help with your work? If you do, don't worry, you're not alone. My name is Emily Cunningham and I'm a writer and literary mentor. I work closely with my colleague and editor, Lorna Howarth who founded The Write Factor publishing agency. Together we support writers in all aspects of their craft through our Absolute Beginners Writing Courses and via our mentoring and coaching sessions. We hit upon the idea of a literary 'Agony Aunt' as a way of increasing the outreach of our work, and for more than two years, I have been writing The Mentor column for Writers' Forum magazine, based on real queries from real writers. This book is a collection of those features, and here's how we think it could help you."

Emily Cunningham, BUDE, CORNWALL

Writing is usually a solitary occupation. Sometimes that's the glory of it. Picture the scene: you're holed-up in your garret, in complete silence apart from the sound of quill scratching parchment and it's absolute bliss being far from the madding crowd, with just your craft for company. Well, that's the romantic view of it, just add a flowing gown or tailcoat and the stereotype will be complete. The reality, of course, is quite different, with the seclusion feeling more like isolation and the peace feeling more like boredom. More time is spent examining your fingernails or monitoring the local starling population than filling page after page of foolscap.

It's all too easy to grind to a halt, and there are a million reasons why this happens: sometimes you hit a thorny problem with your plot that you can't see a way around, or perhaps you've lost faith in your ability to tell a yarn – to name just two scenarios – and that's exactly when a mentor could be choppered-in. Or, more easily, when you can open the pages of this book and select any of the 25 scenarios that apply to you.

Recently, novelist Casey O'Connor (that's a pseudonym – all will be explained) found herself in a creative log-jam and sought my colleague Lorna's expertise. 'I remember the very first phone conversation I had with Casey,' Lorna told me. 'She had the bones of a brilliant story but was in a bit of a muddle about how to get it on to the page. She's had a tumultuous life and wanted to write about it but she was very uncertain about implicating family members. There were also potential legal issues involved as she was writing about fostering and adoption. Add to that low self-confidence and she was left staring at a pile of notes with no clear sense of how to move forward.'

Luckily, over the following few months, Lorna was able to help her unpack all these different issues and find a solution. The result? Casey is now a published novelist, having written *Being Bridie: The Diary of an Aspiring Mother*. Lorna added, 'Mentoring worked for Casey because it helped her to think outside the box. She had become entangled in the idea that her story must be autobiographical, but when we discussed how fictionalising it and writing under a pseudonym would liberate her to write freely, it was a 'light-bulb' moment for Casey. Ironically, it was only through fiction that she could tell the truth.'

This is a great example of what a mentor can do: provide both a different perspective and a sounding board for you to bounce ideas off and reinvigorate your writing. When you work with a mentor, there is someone who is totally non-judgmental and supportive guiding you, so in this book, we have sought to unravel some of the most vexatious issues that face all writers and present them in a way that aims to inspire, inform and encourage you – just like a mentor would.

So why not make yourself a cup of coffee, sit down and plunge into whatever topic waves a red flag at you. This book doesn't have to be read from start to finish; it is more of a deep dive at any point into the depths of the writing craft and when you surface, hopefully you will have greater clarity and a fresh approach to your story. At the end of each feature you will also find some easy tips and exercises to ease you back into writing mode.

Enjoy the journey!

One

WRITING AS THERAPY

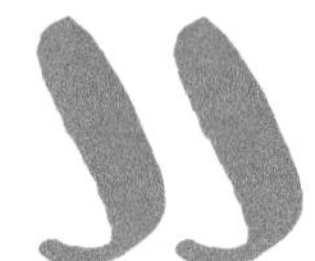

John, COLCHESTER

I want to turn your letter upside-down and give you a completely different view on it. Instead of worrying that your feelings of insecurity and lack of confidence are affecting your writing, why not say: let your writing be the solution to your self-esteem issues? When you have had negative experiences in the past it can be tempting to metaphorically lock the door on them and throw away the key, but, writing about the things that trouble you can often help lay them to rest. Writing as a therapeutic tool has a long-established reputation. It can be a safe way to express emotions and also help clarify them. As Graham Greene said:

> **'Writing is a form of therapy; sometimes I wonder how all those who do not write, compose or paint can manage to escape the madness, melancholia, the panic and fear which is inherent in a human situation.'**

Lorna, my colleague at The Write Factor, is an experienced writing mentor and says that a helpful method to move forward from painful experiences is to name them and incorporate them into your writing practice. For example, if a nagging internal voice is saying: 'Why did my father feel the need to put me down at every opportunity?' ask that question in your writing: construct characters and a dialogue around it, perhaps between a father and his adult son. Explore the feelings from as many different angles as possible. You don't have to justify your feelings or your response to this writing exercise, but just allow whatever pours forth to have its say. You may find that a new understanding emerges, or that the inner voice dissipates.

If the idea of writing about your innermost feelings is too raw, try approaching them in the 'third person' – by which you use pronouns such as he, him, his, himself, she, her, hers, herself, it, its, itself, they, them, their, theirs and themselves, rather than the I/me/we perspective. This removes you from the situation and gives you another, almost voyeuristic, perspective from which to explore the problem. Create some flawed characters who reflect people who you have had difficulty with in reality and make them act out scenarios. For example, a negative mother could become an irritable doctor and your childhood self could become the patient. Give them dialogue and see where it leads. The safety of the page can let you examine traumatic experiences from a distance. As Gillie Bolton, an expert in therapeutic writing says:

> **'Paper's always there to reread or rewrite. Once you've said something you can't unsay it, but with a page of writing you can. You don't ever have to share it. You can burn it if you want.'**

During the process, you always remain in control and can stop for a while and return to it later, as the mood takes you. Getting it out onto the page can also help neutralise some of the power of unhappy memories. As Lorna says, 'A haunting voice needs exorcising. Tease it out from the tangle of your subconscious and tell it to get it out of your life. As this can be a really scary thing to do in reality, do it in your writing instead. These thoughts and feelings, although troubling, are familiar; they have been part of you for so long that you can begin to believe in this narrative, but it is also possible to construct a new narrative that moves beyond where you currently feel stuck. Be playful and imaginative: think outside the box you find yourself in. You may find that this act of imagination is enough to relinquish the power of unhappy memories.'

It's also worth remembering as you write that everyone has insecurities, but if you examine them deeply, they are potentially fascinating stories. People who acknowledge their darker sides tend to write the most interesting prose. Gillie Bolton's own experiences gave weight to her research findings, as she explains in an article in *The Guardian*. 'I suffered some very traumatic experiences, and writing saved my sanity. In my early thirties, I was in a bad psychological state, but didn't really know why. My husband suggested that I write my autobiography. I did, conjuring up a lovely, glorious story. Then I came up with something far more chaotic but closer to the truth. Then, I refined it again, this time into poetry. It's not just the first cathartic outpouring that matters, it's the redrafting. I came to understand what had happened to me only through doing this.'

So it's not just the process of writing that can be therapeutic, it is also the end product – you've written something you're proud of. Whitbread-nominated novelist Jill Dawson recognised this stepping-stone effect. She has kept a journal since she was nine and says: 'It has helped me personally and also made me a better writer, because going over and over something eventually makes it clearer. A dream you don't understand may make sense two years later. Obviously, it undergoes radical transformation before it becomes writing that you would want published, but it is a part of the process. You can find feelings by writing in this raw way that you can then explore using different events in a story.'

Writing as therapy can boost your physical health too. Research at the University of Texas has shown that getting your thoughts down on paper for 20 minutes three times a week will increase the body's immune system functioning. It has also been shown to help with lowering blood pressure, asthma and arthritis.

So, to return to your letter, John, you feel that your childhood has negatively affected your writing and I would like to reassure you that the act of writing itself can help heal emotional wounds and eventually improve your writing ability as you become more attuned to translating your feelings into prose. F. Scott Fitzgerald can't be wrong:

'In short, you have only your emotions to sell. This is the experience of all writers.'

Try this

» Start keeping a diary or journal to get you into the habit of writing. 'Woke up, went to work, had tea,' is a start, but try to focus on your mood. Sometimes just writing it down is enough to let it go. Another bonus of a journal is that you can look back over past entries and remind yourself how far you have come.

» Try a 'mind dump'. Just write randomly for 10 minutes allowing anything to come out and if nothing is forthcoming then kick-start it with word association. It's surprising how this can feel like a mental clear-out.

» Stick this quote by philosopher Jean-Francois Lyotard above your desk for inspiration: *'We write before knowing what to say and how to say it, and in order to find out, if possible.'*

» Try these writing exercises as a springboard into therapeutic writing: write about the future you want, be imaginative: what can you really achieve? Write your story: what happened that keeps you stuck in a cycle of doubt and anxiety? Write a letter to your teenage self: what advice would you give yourself now you are older?

Notes

Two
FINDING INSPIRATION

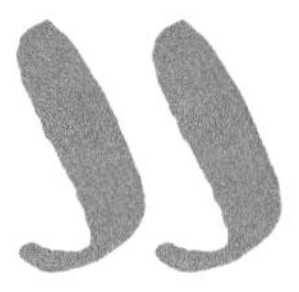

Julie, BARNSTAPLE

What about a story about a writer seeking inspiration? I jest, but there's a nugget of truth in this joke. Potential ideas are all around us, even in the most humdrum places, you just have to get your eye in to spot them. Instead of being a passive observer, try to view life from a writerly standpoint. A useful starting point is to imagine 'what if...?' So if we were to use your problem as an example, perhaps the story could involve a writer who was so desperate for ideas that she started creating dramas in real life to write about? Or, someone whose life started emulating her work, so events only happened to her if she wrote about them?

It's possible to come up with something from nothing if you start thinking laterally. I'm reminded of the book I read recently: *The Truth about the Harry Quebert Affair* by Joel Dicker, which has the central theme of life imitating art and vice versa. The story starts with a young novelist who is suffering from writer's block – I wonder where he got that idea from?

So although at the moment the 'ideas well' seems dry and you're scratching around in the dust, just changing your perspective will transform it into a fount of inspiration. The wrong number you just received could be the start of a wonderful love affair; the dull business meeting you had to endure is a great opportunity for a character study; it's all out there, just waiting to be described and embellished. As Graham Greene said:

'The great advantage of being a writer is that you can spy on people. You're there, listening to every word, but part of you is observing. Everything is useful to a writer, you see – every scrap, even the longest and most boring of luncheon parties.'

My colleague Lorna agrees that writing from life is a rich seam. 'I have found over the years that most people want to write about their life story: it is what they know best (and the old adage, 'write what you know' applies here), but it is also what inspires them to write in the first place. So many people live extraordinary lives and, in many cases, fact is stranger than fiction. Sometimes, at the heart of the desire to write about their lives (their inspiration) is the cathartic need to tell their story; to express what has happened to them in such a way that it might help others to deal with similar situations, or indeed inspire others to experience what they have – especially in terms of adventure or travel writing.' Pick out some of the emotional highs and lows of your life, Julie, and use them as the springboard for fiction.

As well as your own experience, other people's experiences are a valuable resource too. Eavesdropping is a goldmine; try hopping on a bus simply to listen-in to another conversation. It's an amazing source of natural dialogue and also gives you a glimpse at a whole new worldview that you couldn't have begun to imagine. You could also try Googling 'overheard in Waitrose' for a ticklish look at middle-class conversations. Whilst we're on the subject of Googling and the internet, as well as being a wonderful distraction (as Graham Linehan said: 'the problem with a computer is that it is a typewriter hooked up to an everything machine') – it's also a window on the world. You can find such a huge array of different writing styles, perspectives, biographies, it's bound to suggest something to you. Forums and blogs are a great place to sneak a peek into another life, just remember to bear in mind that you're idea-hunting, rather than just reading for enjoyment!

The key to success is that you have to remain aware that you're on the hunt – keep in the forefront of your mind the question: 'How could I turn this into a story?' Ideas can be hidden in plain sight, it's just a matter of noticing them. As Neil Gaiman said:

'You get ideas from daydreaming. You get ideas from being bored. You get ideas all the time. The only difference between writers and other people is we notice when we're doing it.'

Whilst it's important to look at the practical ways of addressing your issue, I think there's an underlying psychological element going on that needs examining. You say that you don't have a problem with maintaining momentum (which is impressive and should be celebrated) but struggle with the first seeds of ideas. Could it be that you don't feel your ideas are interesting and you dismiss them before they have a chance to grow? I think we all underestimate the value of our experiences, so I would encourage you to take a second look at previously discarded ideas. Finally, it's always easier to do something for someone else rather than yourself, so imagine you are running a writing course yourself and come up with exercises for your students.

I hope these suggestions have given you food for thought, Julie – your letter inspired me to explore lots of different avenues whilst answering it, so thank you!

Try this

- » Set yourself the challenge of noticing 'found prose', or unusually lyrical sections in normally prosaic settings. For example, the definition of 'it' in *The Concise Oxford Dictionary* reads like a poem: '*It rains, it is cold; so it seems; it is winter; it is Ash Wednesday, it is Ash Wednesday today; it is 6 o'clock; it is 6 miles to Oxford; it says in the Bible (the Bible says) that all men are liars; I would go if it were not for the expense. It is absurd talking like that; it is incredible that he should refuse; it is a dirty business, this meat-canning; is it difficult to learn Greek? It was a purse that he dropped; it was the Russians that began it.*'

- » Try freewriting – or writing nonstop on anything and everything that pops into your mind – the literary equivalent of a stream of consciousness. This will help you avoid the stumbling blocks of self-criticism and fear of being boring.

- » Don't wrangle with this for too long, as Dan Poynter said: 'If you wait for inspiration to write, you're not a writer, you're a waiter.'

Notes

Three
WRITING FROM LIFE

"I am experimenting with basing my characters on real people in my novel but wondered whether this is acceptable? I don't mean legally, as I'm aware of libel laws, I'm more concerned about the ethics of it. What do you think?"

Paul, LIVERPOOL

This is a very interesting question, Paul, because writers often have a bad reputation due to their habit of sniffing around people like bloodhounds, always in search of good material, almost disregarding the feelings of the person in favour of the story. Like journalists, writers have to gather information in order to fill their pages and it's this necessity that makes friends and family quake in their boots. Every time a novel is published, each word is scrutinised by the people the writer knows, looking to see if they can recognise themselves in it.

As a journalist myself, I have been guilty of listening to a friend recount an anecdote and my eyes glazing over as I turn their experience into a potential feature pitch in my head, complete with headline. For example, when a friend's baby was discovered to have numerous, life-threatening food allergies, the headline 'Thank goodness for bananas' popped into my head and I promptly asked if I could interview her for an article. Luckily, she was amenable to this, but surely my first impulse should be concern, not journalistic potential?

I suppose the difference lies in what our priorities are and whether can they coexist at the same time. Is it more important to be a sympathetic friend or a good writer? I think it's possible to be both. You can treat a friend with sensitivity and still gain inspiration from their lives. After all, what else do we have to draw on but the lives of others (and our own)?

This approach is beautifully illustrated by PD James who, when asked for advice on writing fiction, said:

'Open your mind to new experiences, particularly to the study of other people. Nothing that happens to a writer – however happy, however tragic – is ever wasted.'

The difference between being the literary equivalent of a circling vulture and a discreet observer is how you use the information – and this is key: to avoid causing offence, upset and even litigation, you have to make your characters completely unrecognisable. In a fascinating article: *'How to offend Nobody'* by Randy Ingermanson (www.advancedfictionwriting.com) he says, 'I've only ever had one person ask me if a character was based on him. My answer was no. I had taken one of his major traits and used it for a particular character and I told him that. But I also said that I don't ever base a character completely on any one person. I take a bit of this and a bit of that from different people, and a lot of it I just make up. And usually, each of my main characters gets at least one major trait from me. That ensures that I can write that character realistically from the inside.'

To move further still from reality, my colleague Lorna also recommends that you identify the bones of the story behind the anecdote and look at what the universal truth is that is speaking to you: Betrayal? Loss? Death? Focus on the heart of the matter to depart from what actually happened. Lorna was reminded of a recent manuscript she worked on about the excesses of the 1960s, set in swinging London. Since it was loosely based on the reminiscences of the writer, she had become constrained by this and produced a completely linear narrative that read like an autobiography. Lorna advised her to return to her work and view it as a novel. 'I suggested she weave subplots into the warp and weft of the story, and introduce different voices and events to help her move away from reality.' Staying doggedly loyal to how the events actually unfolded is inadvisable, not just because of libel, but because it's often boring. As Clive James said:

**'Fiction is life with the dull bits
left out.'**

Writing about yourself can also be very cathartic but to make it fiction, instead of writing about your miserable childhood with a domineering father, you can literally rewrite history to transform yourself into a child prodigy with a proud father: this is both therapeutic and unidentifiable. Constantly examine your motives to ensure your moral compass remains true north. 'Your work must come from a place of integrity, not from retribution or revenge,' says Lorna. 'It's tempting to turn an ex-partner into the villain of the piece, and this may be a form of catharsis, but it's also morally dubious if you plan to have it in the public domain. Always remember that everyone, however loathsome you find them, has rights and these must be respected. Never say anything in a story that you wouldn't say face to face.'

So, in answer to your question, Paul, I would heed the words of A L Kennedy:

'You can, of course, steal stories and attributes from family and friends, fill in file cards after lovemaking and so forth. [But] It might be better to celebrate those you love – and love itself – by writing in such a way that everyone keeps their privacy and dignity intact.'

Try this

» Make the phrase 'This is fiction' your new mantra.

» Try this writing exercise. Start with a real event that has recently happened – for example, a friend's house being flooded – as the starting point and then turn it on its head. What's the opposite of a flood? A fire? A drought? Perhaps your character could be stuck in the desert in a broken-down jeep? Disguising who your characters are based on can be an interesting exercise to test your imagination.

» Always keep W B Yeats' comment in mind when you're lifting ideas from other people's lives: 'Tread softly because you tread on my dreams.' In other words, be sensitive to the feelings of others.

Notes

Four

WHAT IS 'SHOW NOT TELL'?

"I keep hearing the phrase: 'Show not tell' with regards to writing, but I'm not exactly sure what it means. Surely all writing is 'telling'?"

Anders, SOUTH SHIELDS

Funnily enough, Anders, my first-ever student on the Absolute Beginners Writing Course that I run had this same conundrum. The concept of 'showing not telling' was covered in the first session and she couldn't get her head around it. I agree that it's a slippery one, so I will endeavour to explain. 'Showing and not telling' is pretty much a mantra for editors and writing tutors these days. The reason why such importance is placed on this skill is because it can really enhance narration, characterisation, context and scene-setting. In short, becoming proficient in the ability to show not tell can radically improve the standard of your work.

But how, I hear you ask. Well, rather than listing your character's physical attributes and history – 'telling' us about her (she had blue eyes and red hair) – your prose should 'show' us who she is via the context, her actions, dialogue and the experience of being in her mind and body (she pulled a strand of her auburn hair hating the way the sun turned it orange; her anger making her eyes spark sapphire blue). Rather than setting out your store in one go in terms of telling (this happened and then that happened), showing helps your readers to get to know your characters more naturally because it allows them to enter into the char-

acter's worldview. I hope that's a little clearer than mud, Anders? Stick with me as we delve into this further.

Writer Sharon Zink (*Welcome to Sharonville*), says, 'It's important to not "tell" emotions – like the shock and terror one might experience when being attacked, for example. In this case, showing would mean really getting into how the victim experiences this emotion in his body and interior monologue. What does he think, feel and do? This immerses the reader more fully into his experience of being attacked, thus helping us to identify with the character, making the action have more impact overall.'

Sharon goes on to say, 'Telling is never as vivid as showing, so if something is important to your plot, such as an argument or accident, slow the scene down and really show the reader the protagonist's sweat and high heart rate or however he/she personally experiences terror. Remember that every character will experience emotion differently – some people shout when they're angry, whilst others eat ice cream and simmer in silence, so explore deeply how your characters specifically 'do' feeling and show the reader how this mani- fests for them.'

So how does showing, not telling affect narration? Consider, for example, the overwhelming force involved in a car accident and how actually showing this event as it happens or, better still, how it is *experienced* by your lead, will be a more powerful way of depicting the violence of this crash. Telling often results in rushing over key events, but showing helps you to really make the most of the drama of your plot and allows the emotions and significance of what has happened hit home for your reader.

> **'Some people shout when they're angry, whilst others eat ice cream and simmer in silence, so explore deeply how your characters specifically 'do' feeling and show the reader how this manifests for them.'**

We return to Sharon again: 'It's important to show, not tell, when describing a novel's settings. You may state for example that there are "elegant" roads and "imposing" houses, but these words mean different things to different people, so if you really want your readers to see the affluence and beauty of a neighbourhood, you need to show specific details of the houses and street, using the senses, such as sounds, sights, tastes and smells, so the location really comes over clearly.'

So far, showing is being portrayed as more effective than telling, but the latter does have its place as an effective tool in writing and is not to be sniffed at – it moves the plot on and is vital for exposition. Once you've got your eye in, it's easy to spot some very clunky examples of telling in detective shows where, once the villain is captured, they explain the whole plot. But the problem with overusing telling is that it can become boring. The detective show's plots would be much more elegant if the audience could work it out for themselves. Telling can be used skilfully and effectively in dialogue, for example, where it is absolutely natural for someone to tell their friend what's going on in their life.

When you're writing early drafts of a book, it's easy to want to plough forward and just get the action down, but that is the time to really look in detail at the manuscript and sharpen your skills of showing, not telling so your story concept can be conveyed effectively.

As well as bringing depth, colour and emotion to the piece, showing also makes the reader think and really exercise their cognitive muscles, which is satisfying. A wonderful example of this was in a book I read recently: *State of Wonder* by Ann Patchett (I actually stopped reading to get a pencil and write it down!). The main character was moved to tears whilst watching an opera as it drew parallels with events in her own life, but the only way the reader knew that she was crying is by another character's actions and comment: 'Barbara opened up her tiny purse and handed Marina a Kleenex. "Blot in a straight line beneath your eyes," she whispered.'

When the penny drops, after a skilful piece of showing, the reader feels simultaneously included and admiring. It creates a connection between the writer and the reader; an intimacy that is not found in the more neutral and practical telling. In the excellent blog *This Itch of Writing* by Emma Darwin (emmadarwin. typepad.com) she suggests that instead of viewing the two writing techniques as either/ or, you could see them as gradients of the same scale: 'It's often quoted as "Show, don't tell" because, on the whole, beginner writers do too much telling when they should be showing. But of course it's not nearly as simple as that. Both have their value; the key is to understand their respective strengths, and use each to your story's best advantage.

Mind you, like everything in writing, it isn't even binary, but a spectrum, from the telliest tell, to the showiest show.'

So whilst you're right that all writing is telling, showing is more about the style than the content, breathing life into a story so that the reader fully engages with it and, if only for a moment, joins the characters on their adventures. I hope I have helped you crystallise these ideas, and inspire you to try a little showing not telling of your own.

Try this

- » Use the 'show not tell' technique to illustrate the sentence: 'It was hot.'

- » Using all the five senses to describe something is an easy way to develop your 'showing' skills. Try doing this to write about where you are sitting right now.

- » Start with a simple 'tell' sentence such as: 'He was angry' and gradually build on it in five stages so it becomes a 'show' sentence. You will see how the emotional distance between the reader and the action grows closer with each stage.

Notes

Five
CREATING CHARACTERS

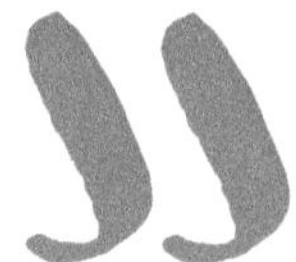

Wendy, NORWICH

As you've realised, creating realistic characters that the reader invests in emotionally, is central to a successful story. You can have a gripping plot with incredible twists and turns, but if the reader doesn't care about what happens to the characters then it's all for naught. Imagine if Heathcliff was a dullish, fair-to-middling sort of man – Cathy wouldn't be bothered either way if he came back to claim her and neither would the reader.

Luckily, one of the easiest places to start is just a short step away from writing about yourself – something you already are comfortable with – and that is drawing on the characters of people you know. When you imagine a relative, you can easily hear their voice and have access to a wide repertoire of the phrases and vocabulary they use. My father-in-law, coming from Yorkshire, often calls me, 'Emily love' and just conjuring-up him saying those words lets me easily imagine other dialogue in his voice.

Use this trick as a stepping-stone for fleshing out your characters. Choose a key phrase that defines them to help you imagine exactly who they are – their background, their age, appearance, motivation. When you have outlined them in broad strokes, go deeper to really get under their skin. What is their temperament? Strident? Affectionate? Passionate?

Next, it's key to get your characters' names just right – spend time researching the meaning and exploring all different variants. 'Vera' as a name feels very different to 'Vicki'. Choose carefully as names are powerful signifiers. They also need to be in keeping with both the era and the person – although beware of insulting stereotypes. Whilst you may pick 'Chardonnay' to name a shop worker, it may be considered slightly contemptuous. Would you call a barrister by the same name?

Dickens was particularly good at choosing names – practically every single character had a memorable name that reflected its owner's personality, such as Volumnia Dedlock and Wackford Squeers. You could even make up a name, like Shakespeare did or popularise a rare one, like JM Barrie did with your own name – Wendy, in *Peter Pan*.

After you've got the name nailed, move on to the way your characters speak – one character could have a good sense of humour, or a love of bad puns whilst another could be fond of talking in clichés. Be sure to notice what they *don't* say as much as what they do. For example, how the maternal character always asks after others but never mentions her own wellbeing. When you have built up a consistent pattern of speech for each character then you can start to have fun by subverting it. At times of crisis people behave unpredictably and so long as you have set up a firm foundation of who they are, then it's exciting for them to act 'out of character'.

Then, take a look at how they move the plot forward. Your characters are the pivot around which the action happens. Novelist and screen-writer Maria Semple says:

'I keep an elaborate calendar for my characters detailing on which dates everything happens. I'm constantly revising this as I go along. It gives me the freedom to intricately plot my story, knowing it will at least hold up on a timeline.'

Creating a personal schedule for each char-acter like this just shows the lengths to which writers go, not only to make their characters believable, but also to ensure the intricacies of plot, timeline and backstory stack-up. It may seem daunting but in fact you can just view it as having a systematic approach, rather than just hoping for the best.

The words that your characters say describe not just their personalities but their points of view, their perspectives on the world. To distinguish clearly between different char-acters, make sure that they react differently to things. Whilst one may walk into a room and immediately notice their surroundings, including temperature and ambience, another could be completely oblivious, reflecting their different sensitivities.

Contrasting characters' reactions can bring different nuances to the same scene and provoke a deeper engagement with the reader. A novel that I recently edited had two characters who shared many of the same characteristics – driven, arrogant, egotistical businessmen – and this made the plot dangerously one-dimen-sional. Happily, after some feedback, the author introduced a character who was self-aware and vulnerable and it served as a mirror, reflecting the monstrous personalities of the others. It also brought colour and variety to the piece.

Which brings me to the next point: that characters literally bring the story alive, and thus have an important job to do. Because of this, they need to be vivid and memorable. Thriller writer Ken Follett is well aware of this requirement:

'People are much more complicated in real life, but my characters are as subtle and nuanced as I can make them. But, if you say my charac-ters are too black and white, you've missed the point. Villains are meant to be black-hearted in popular novels. If you say I have a grey-hearted villain, then I've failed.'

Take Ken's approach and make your characters exciting, challenging and thought-provoking. If you want to include an optimist then make them truly sunshiney. Let the reader understand *what* makes them so upbeat and also *why* they are. Once you address these issues, then the characters starts to fizz with energy. Also, a magical thing starts to happen – they move the plot along by themselves. They are no longer puppets but autonomous beings. I love the way John Updike describe this effect:

'Each morning my characters greet me with misty faces willing, though chilled, to muster for another day's progress through the dazzling quicksand, the marsh of blank paper.'

There's lots of fun to be had with the creation of new characters, Wendy, and I hope I've given you some inspiration to get started with.

Try this

» To help your characters come alive, give them homework that won't be used in the piece. Make them write a letter or even just a tweet to get to grips with how they express themselves.

» When writing your character's dialogue, read it out loud and include inflections and mannerisms to really get into their mind-set. As Vladimir Nabokov said: 'I shall not exist if you do not imagine me.'

» Gain inspiration and realistic dialogue by eavesdropping. Snatches of conversation can be rich pickings for your story.

Notes

Six
CELEBRATING THE MUNDANE

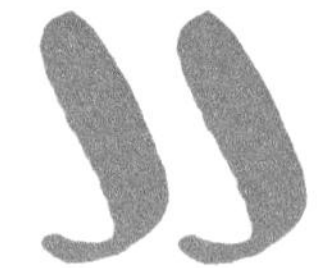

Julian, CROMER

It's only a problem if you perceive it as such, Julian. You're right that traditionally, the exciting twists and turns of plot development and narrative arc are what creates a page-turner but it is possible to produce an absorbing read without these usual devices. A fresh and unique example of this is Nicholson Baker's book *The Mezzanine*. He uses lengthy footnotes on almost every page to take the reader on fascinating diversions. For example, he discusses at length the most effective way to fill an ice cube tray with water – should the tap be aimed at each section in turn or just one, allowing the water to overflow into the others? Who would have thought that reading about such minutiae of life could be interesting, but it is.

I think his success is based on the fact that he makes observations about everyday activities that we normally do without thinking. In sociology, these events are described as 'seen but unnoticed'. By drawing our attention to them, he manages to bring them into sharp focus, a subject for consideration, much in the same way many stand-up comedians start their jokes with:

'Have you ever noticed...?' They get laughs by pointing out familiar behaviour that we all recognise but have never stopped to think about.

So it's definitely an acceptable and appealing style of writing and, as a bonus, it's also all the rage. My colleague, Lorna, agrees: 'I've noticed in publishing that books that lack the usual narrative arc and that are really just an exquisite meditation on life, are 'trending' at the moment. These books and stories 'acclaim the mundane,' meaning that the narrative arc is not the key driver of the book – although some do have a traditional beginning, middle and end with a denouement at some point.'

So your writing needn't be action-packed to be riveting. It's a good example of when 'style over content' needn't be a criticism. Lorna continues: 'With the trend in mundanity, which is not meant in any way to be a derogatory term but which gives a flavour of 'everydayness', what raises these books to exception (although some do miss the mark) is the acute attention to detail, where observation, descriptive prowess and lyrical turns of phrase are enough to carry the book.'

A recent bestseller that ticks all these boxes is *My Name is Lucy Barton* by Elizabeth Strout. In essence, not much happens in the book, but what makes it such a superb read is the way the author reflects on how the protagonist, the eponymous Lucy, pieces together the details of a childhood that was so deprived, she didn't even realise it was until her mother is in hospital, dying, and they speak for the first time about all that has been swept under the carpet. It is set over a period of five days and the listlessness of being in a hospital; the incompleteness of memory; the frustration at her taciturn mother all combine to create a novel that is rather marvellous in its mundanity.

Perhaps the lesson to be taken from this is that ordinary lives – the everydayness of them, the mundanity – are endlessly fascinating to other people. What we think of as possibly boring and in need of fictionalising, can in fact be revelatory to another.

To bring up the dreaded Facebook, I have often thought that an excellent salve against all the boasting and 'look at me' egotism would be to post about ordinary days, nothing-to-write-home-about views and bog-standard meals. Instead of the usual photo of a spectacular view from someone's holiday balcony, I'd relish the sight of a dull picture of a garden wall. Jacket potato and beans instead of a seafood platter. There's something so refreshing about celebrating the normal, and grounding too. It's an excellent weapon in the constant battle against feeling inadequate.

There's no need to measure yourself against others who may be writing thrillers or action adventures – your own contribution is likely to be just as engaging on another level. There's also more than just a tinge of mindfulness about this perspective. Instead of rushing from one murder/abduction/sex scene to the next, you can stop and smell the roses (and look at their velvety texture). You are allowing your readers to pause for a moment to truly experience something authentic and honest, instead of giving them a quick thrill.

There's even scientific research to support this. A study by Harvard Business School in 2014 discovered that whilst our phones are full of those photos recording red-letter days, it's the humdrum, normal pictures that strike a special chord. We underestimate the pleasure that these often overlooked snaps give us. In the same way, your quiet approach does not have the same razzmatazz but brings a wonderful contentment and peace.

As Lorna says: 'For the aspiring writer, the lesson is – as Lucy Barton's own creative writing teacher tells her when she is struggling to find her writer's voice: "You will have only one story… You'll write your one story many ways. Don't ever worry about story. You will have only one." By which she means, your one story, which may result in a dozen books, can only be one story ultimately, and that's your story. It's an inspiring way to unleash your imagination because nobody else in the entire world can tell your story.' Never underestimate what you have to offer, Julian.

'Nobody else in the entire world can tell your story.'

Try this

» To fine-tune your descriptive skills, write about the view from your window but make sure it's a dull one. You could even take it up a notch in the humdrum stakes and turn your attention to the window itself instead of the view from it. PVC? Tell me more!

» For an example of style over content taken to the nth degree, try reading *Exercises in Style* by Raymond Queneau, in which he rewrites just one event – an argument on a bus – 99 different ways.

» Try the mindfulness meditation practise of eating a raisin. You can't just pop it in though, take your time over it. The whole thing must take several minutes. First you must examine it closely, then smell it, savour it in your mouth before finally chewing it. Immerse yourself in the full experience of 'raisinness' and then write about it.

Notes

Seven
READING WHILE WRITING

Evan, ABERDEEN

I can see what you mean Evan – there is always a fear that somehow your own voice may be diluted if you hear or read other writers during the creative process. The power of a beautifully written book is such that it *does* get inside your head – it's hard to put down and when you do, you can't stop thinking about it, so it makes sense to worry that it may contaminate your own creative waters. In an effort to prevent this, I can see the appeal of adopting a purist mentality of forbidding any outside noise to affect you when you're in the writing zone.

There are other benefits to focusing purely on your own writing, too – for one, reading is incredibly distracting. If you're in the middle of a page-turner, time put aside for writing can quickly become swallowed-up if you pick up that book again. It is also an excellent form of procrastination, especially if you declare to yourself that it is actually 'research'. While research has its place, overly long spent on it is, in truth, just another way of not applying yourself to the task in hand, along with suddenly getting the urge to trim your nails and eradicate dandelions from the garden. One friend admitted she found herself cleaning her radio with a toothbrush to avoid writing, which is definitely a step too far.

The main reason, as you point out, is the possibility that your style may become corrupted. As writer Zoë Heller said: 'Some novelists I know abstain from reading other people's fiction when they are writing their own, for fear of adulterating their prose style with unconscious borrowings. The rigour of this impresses me. (The rules and habits of other writers invariably seem worthier and wiser than mine.)'

However, she then goes on to make a very good observation about the numerous benefits to be found from reading while writing: 'I don't have the discipline to forswear fiction for the years that it takes me to finish a book. And in any case, I'm not entirely convinced that having another author's style rub off on mine would be such a terrible thing.'

I like Heller's modesty and honesty here. The advantages of reading other writers' work are enormous, especially if you are still finding your feet in the literary world. As my colleague Lorna pointed out: 'When we read, we subconsciously absorb all the building blocks that make up a good book; the narrative arc, how dialogue affects a scene, creating a sub-plot. Without these, we struggle to write effectively.' Or, as Ben Okri said:

'Reading, like writing, is a creative act. If readers only bring a narrow range of themselves to the book, then they'll only see a narrow range reflected in it.'

Having a comprehensive understanding of literature in all its forms engages us with the publishing world – the different trends and genres – and with this education comes a confidence that is evident when we write. I recently provided a manuscript assessment and it quickly became apparent that the author had not read widely, particularly within his genre. I could see the potential for an interesting piece of work but what was lacking was a recognition of the attributes of his genre – pace, drama, tension. I feel he would have been more aware of what was missing from his work had he read similar works by published authors. I might dare to say that reading is *vital* to producing work of any quality. As Stephen King says, and I wouldn't want to contradict *him*:

'If you don't have time to read, you don't have the time (or the tools) to write.'

As well as showing us the rules, published writers also show how to break them. Eimar McBride, inspired by reading *Ulysses*, threw away the rulebook when she wrote *A Girl is a Half-formed Thing*, an emotionally charged stream of consciousness with erratic punctuation and fractured sentences. Both my colleague Lorna and I admitted that if she had approached us, we would have hesitated to publish her book at The Write Factor because of its unconventional format – in the words of David Collard, 'a prose which deploys a spartan lexicon in fragmentary vernacular syncopations' – and other publishers were equally reluctant. For nine years it languished in her drawer until finally, she succeeded in getting it published by Faber & Faber and went on to win the Baileys Women's Prize for Fiction in 2014, which just shows that being motivated by others and daring to take risks can pay dividends.

If we take a step back from the nuts and bolts of writing, there are more abstract benefits too. When we read, we think, percolate and process, and when we write, these contemplations crystallise and become a resource to be used on the page.

A beautiful quote that illustrates just how closely connected the two are, is by Pam Allyn:

'Reading is like breathing in; writing is like breathing out.'

Finally, it also helps keep the creative spark alight. Don't worry about the risk of imitation, just revel in the joy that a good book brings. Ralph Waldo Emerson got it right when he said: 'I cannot remember the books I've read any more than the meals I have eaten; even so, they have made me.' Reading nourishes us, so don't hesitate to enjoy one book while writing another.

Try this

- » Take a break from your work to try this exercise – it may help you clarify how much your own style comes through. Read a paragraph of a book by a novelist with a distinctive style, such as Bill Bryson or James Joyce and then write a paragraph in their style. Now rewrite the paragraph in your own style and compare the two. This simple act will hopefully show you that bringing your own colour to the piece has far more value than aping another person's style.

- » Remember that first and foremost you are sharing *your* thoughts and they are unique. If you keep this uppermost in your mind, your work will ring true.

- » Leave your literary comfort zone by reading outside your preferred genre – it will open your eyes to the variety of writing styles out there and may inspire you too.

- » One of my favourite is *Writing Down the Bones – Freeing the Writer Within*, by Natalie Goldberg. She reflects on her own efforts to write in such an uplifting, encouraging way that you can't help but be inspired.

Notes

Eight

NOVELISTS INTIMIDATE ME

"How can I possibly even think of picking up a pen when there is such a wealth of incredible literature out there already? I look back at my efforts and feel so disheartened because they seem so poor compared to my favourite authors – especially Neil Gaiman's work. Is there any point to writing when I can't compete?"

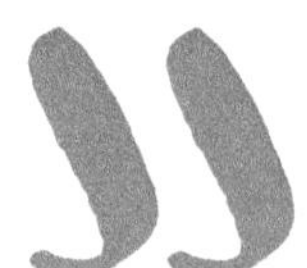

Sophie, BASINGSTOKE

The thought that sprang to my mind when I read your letter was Theodore Roosevelt's great quote: 'Comparison is the thief of joy.' It's so true; you can be perfectly happy writing and feeling pleased with what you've produced and then just one negative thought: 'It's not Shakespeare, though, is it?' and all your hard work seems for naught. The human mind can be at once so creative and so destructive.

Joan Didion, author of *The Year of Magical Thinking*, was similarly afflicted when she read the work of Henry James:

'He wrote perfect sentences [...] Very indirect, very complicated. Sentences *with* sinkholes. You could drown in them. I wouldn't dare to write one. I'm not even sure I'd dare to read James again. I loved those novels so much that I was paralysed by them for a long time. All those possibilities. All that perfectly reconciled style. It made me afraid to put words down.'

Happily for us readers, she did dare to write, and in such a unique and refreshing way too – nothing like Henry James, and still brilliant. Equally, your work probably does not resemble Neil Gaiman's but that's not to say that it isn't good. The great thing about a creative endeavour is that it isn't a competition; everyone has something to offer. Mr Gaiman himself, in his inspiring speech at The University of the Arts, recognises the value of new voices:

'The urge, starting out, is to copy. And that's not a bad thing. Most of us only find our own voices after we've sounded like a lot of other people. But the one thing that you have that nobody else has is *you*. Your voice, your mind, your story, your vision.'

So, Sophie, what you have to offer is unique – celebrate it. Wanting to be like other writers is like aspiring to be an orange when you're an apple. It's fruitless (sorry). Neither is better

– both have their merits in different ways. Instead, take courage from Gaiman's words; you *can* be a trail-blazing writer, you *can* carve out your own path. You have something valuable to give. At the moment, this is hard to recognise, but I promise you, it is there.

When I mentioned your letter to my colleague Lorna, she was reminded of an experience when she was younger: 'I found learning to drive such a struggle. I'd look at people driving so easily and think: "That will never be me. I can't do this. I'm never going to pass my test." And I failed, four times. But I learnt such a lot from the process of failure and I did eventually pass. Now I *can* drive, my perspective is so different: I know I'm a good driver. Driving had felt like an impossible dream. Now it's a breeze. To quote Nelson Mandela, "It always seems impossible until it is done."'

When we're struggling, we deafen ourselves with negative self-talk. We compare ourselves to others and find ourselves lacking and inferior. How is this in any way helpful? Instead of harsh judgment, try to view your writing more kindly. At least you *are* writing, which is a lot more than can be said of most people. I recently worked on a client's first draft of a novel, and although there was still work to be done before it was ready for publication, overall, I was still hugely impressed with the fact that he had written 130,000 words of original prose.

Ernest Hemingway, never known for being backward in coming forward, said:

'The first draft of anything is shit.'

When you're reading Neil Gaiman's books, don't forget that they have all been through a very thorough editing process. They've probably changed vastly from the first thoughts he put down on paper. Also, as well as within a novel, his writing ability has evolved and improved over the course of several novels. He himself said: 'Sometimes the things I did really didn't work. There are stories of mine that have never been printed. Some of them never even left the house. But I learned as much from them as I did from the things that worked.' Gaiman persisted, and his writing improved until he was an internationally acclaimed writer. It didn't happen overnight but he kept on trying because that was what he wanted to do.

A brilliant post on the website www.writersincharge.com by Thuy Yau really hits the nail on the head about feelings of inadequacy. She used to describe herself as an 'aspiring writer' until she had an epiphany. 'What was an "aspiring writer" exactly?' she says. 'Going by the literal definition, it would've been someone who wasn't writing *yet*. But was *intending* to write – someday. But wait a minute, I was writing at the time! So how could I have been an "aspiring writer"? And then it hit me. I was a writer! I wasn't getting paid, I wasn't selling books. *But I was writing*. I was writing to help others. I was writing because I wanted to touch lives. That's when my attitude towards writing changed. I started calling myself a "writer". I developed the self-confidence that every writer needs, to be successful. I didn't care anymore that hardly anyone read my blog; I believed in my talents and knew that someday people would believe in them too.'

And now she's being quoted in this book – so look how far she has come.

It's tempting to imagine that published novelists are in an elite, superior realm that is impossibly far above you, but a) they are human too, riddled with self-doubt and insecurity like the rest of us and b) everyone starts somewhere. As good old Mr Hemingway said:

'We are all apprentices in a craft where no one ever becomes the master.'

So enjoy reading your favourite authors, remember that they too struggled at first (and probably still do) and pick up your pen once more.

Try this

» Instead of being intimidated by your favourite novelists, be inspired. What is it about Neil Gaiman that you admire so much? Is it his incredible imagination? Dare to test your own limits. For five minutes, write about the strangest thing that could happen to you – becoming invisible? Discovering a wormhole in the cellar? Inhabiting the mind of a unicorn?

» Push your work the extra mile by making your descriptions really zing. Some fieldwork would help, such as developing your observational skills by going for a walk. Whilst you're out, take a mental note of anything orange then write a short piece that incorporates all the orange things you see.

» Read aloud one of your favourite pieces of writing and feel proud of your accomplishment. Then return to it with an editor's eye: what needs tightening up? Are there any clichés or stereotypes that need rejigging? Rewrite it until it's *even* better (if that's possible).

Notes

Nine
WILL I EVER IMPROVE?

Helen, WAREHAM

Before we begin, I want to reassure you that since I haven't read your work, this is all pure speculation. Please don't be reduced to an empty husk if I imply that you're wasting your time and should take up tapestry instead. For all I know you might be Helen Fielding or Helen Dunmore, in which case, you don't need to improve, you've hit pay dirt.

Obviously I can't judge whether you have improved or not, but it's an interesting concept to look at despite this. There are two ways to approach it: firstly, that you *have* improved but are being too harsh on yourself, which is when I would suggest that you seek others' views on your work for a boost to your self-esteem. Alternatively, we could explore the idea that you are in fact correct. You haven't improved. Before you push over your desk and snap your pencils, don't despair. Wanting to improve is a step in the right direction.

Hanif Kureishi ruffled quite a few feathers when he said (whilst teaching creative writing at Kingston University) that 99.9% of his students were untalented and that writing a story is: 'a difficult thing to do and it's a great skill to have. Can you teach that? I don't think you can.' (I wonder how popular his seminars were after that?) The implication being, since it's impossible to teach good writing, it's impossible to learn it. I disagree. I think this is part of the snobbery of those in the elite group of published authors. Why would they say anyone can learn it? What's in it for them? No, instead they prefer to say you have to be born with an innate talent where perfect prose magically flows onto the page. It's a closed shop and impossible to break into.

Phillip Hensher writing in *The Guardian*, acknowledges this perspective but offers an alternative view: 'Commentators sometimes say that writing can't be taught; that writers either have "it", in which case they don't need to be taught, or they don't have "it", in which case money and time is being wasted by the exercise. But writers can perfectly well have native ability, a feel for language, an inventiveness and a keen eye towards the world and still not quite understand how they can do something well, not once, but repeatedly.'

Hensher goes on to prove this point by using his own work as an example:

'When I look at my first novels, they seem to me to have no idea about technical features of the novel. I don't think I really had a solid novelistic technique until I wrote my third or fourth novel.'

So what is the magic ingredient that transformed Hensher from being technically weak to strong? My colleague Lorna, suggests that it's time. 'Writers benefit from the passing years, much like a good wine or piece of cheese! Age and experience bring a wider perspective on life, one that can see themes and threads of narrative that ebb and flow over the years.' She also goes on to say: 'All crafts are honed; life gives us stories from which we can base our novels and practise makes perfect.'

In essence, it is possible to improve but you have to dedicate time and effort to it. What have you been doing over the years to hone your craft? It's all too easy to fall into a creative rut. Could it be that you aren't stretching yourself? At a writing class that I used to go to, we would be set an exercise and even before beginning it I could predict exactly how some of the other students' work would turn out. They approached every challenge in the same way – same point of view, same tone, same perspective. They had become lazy. Their characters were stereotypes and their dialogue uninventive. If this sounds incredibly mean, instead of feeling cross with me (I am beyond

reproach), use your anger as an incentive not to be that student. Lift your writing up to another level.

But how, how, how? Reading other people's work is one good way. Compare your work to your favourite author's. Bit of an 'ouch' moment, I expect. Now investigate exactly how it differs. Are their sentence structures more elegant? Are their plots more ingenious? Are their characters more vividly drawn? Revisit your work again with the aim of making it the best it can be. Imagine that favourite novelist reading it. Try not to crumple inside, instead rise to the challenge.

Rachel Cusk describes a fascinating technique to make her students stretch themselves: 'The desire to write comes easily; writing itself is technical and hard. I give my students exercises in which a certain object has to feature. I choose the object myself: the more alien it is to their subjective processes the better. The object represents the impingement of reality, and it nearly always has the effect of turning their writing inside out. Over time I've learned which objects work the best: some of the things I've used – a violin, a pair of scissors – have been too easily conscripted into the student's subjective world. Others – a lawnmower, a new pair of shoes – unfailingly make the writing more objective. The narrative has to find a way around it, like water has to flow around an obstacle, and the result is that the whole enterprise is given form.'

Remember, too, that improving doesn't mean sacrificing your own writer's identity. Keep that kernel of promising work and nourish it. Have faith in your own voice and ability and don't consider yourself less than other writers. As Toby Litt said: 'Demystify what "real" writers are. Too many people write badly because they write up to their idea of what "real" writing should be or what a "real" writer should write. They put on literary airs. If someone holds writers in too much esteem, they'll never become one.'

Finally, amidst all this talk of moving forwards, take a moment to celebrate the fact that you have been enjoying creative writing for years. This is an achievement in itself, and should not be forgotten.

Try this

- » Select one of your favourite passages you have written and critique it. What would make it stronger? Try changing it from third to first person (or vice versa). Try reading it aloud. Hold it up to the light and hunt for flaws.

- » If you're feeling brave, swap work with another writer friend and do the above. See what changes they have made. Ask them to explain their reasons (and keep sharp objects out of the room).

- » Try Phillip Hensher's suggestion of dropping a block of frozen urine onto a scene you've written, just to see what would happen. I like the sound of his writing course…

- » Practice stepping outside of yourself to adjust the perspective. One way to do this is to imagine someone you know reading your work – an elderly uncle or your daughter's teacher for example. Try to guess what their reactions would be and what they would and would not enjoy about your work. Learning from this, develop your work so these elements are stronger.

Notes

Ten
HOW DO I IMPROVE MY VOCABULARY?

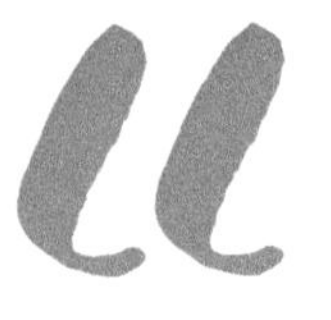

"When I read, I'm always impressed by the author's use of interesting vocabulary but it's also made me aware that my own writing is somewhat lacking because I don't have a wide vocabulary – how can I improve it?"

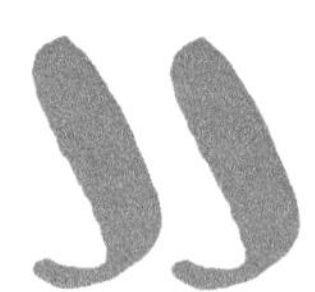

Gareth, KENILWORTH

Apparently, the average person knows 10,000 words but only uses 2,000 of them regularly, so you're not wrong in thinking that on a day-to-day basis our vocabulary is limited. When applying ourselves to creative writing, there is a pressure to sound erudite and pepper our sentences with sesquipedalian words – see, I'm doing it now – but before you reach for the dictionary, let me reassure you that there is beauty in simplicity. Ideas can be expressed clearly and powerfully using basic English. Both *The Old Man and the Sea* and *Animal Farm* are cited as 'easy reads' yet no one would dream of criticising the authors for their lack of flowery language.

Stephen King, in his book *On Writing: A Memoir of the Craft* said:

'One of the really bad things you can do to your writing is to dress up the vocabulary, looking for long words because you're maybe a little bit ashamed of your short ones. This is like dressing up a household pet in evening clothes. The pet is embarrassed and the person who committed this act of premeditated cuteness should be even more embarrassed.'

I love the image of the embarrassed pet and you'll notice that in this quote, the point is made perfectly in plain English, in fact, there's something refreshing about its simplicity.

There is also the danger that crowbarring long words into your work will backfire, in that it ends up putting people off. Howard Mittelmark makes this point hilariously in *How Not to Write a Novel: 200 Classic Mistakes and How to Avoid Them—A Misstep-by-Misstep Guide:* 'When the reader has stopped to wonder at your delamificatious vocabulary, or, worse, when the reader has stopped because the word you've used has no more meaning to him than a random ptliijnbvc of letters, the reader is not involved in your story. Generally, saying "edifice" instead of "building" doesn't tell your reader anything about the building; it tells the reader that you know that word edifice.' And yes, I looked up the word, 'delamificatious', feeling both peeved that I didn't know it and hoping to add it to my vocabulary – it doesn't exist! Point well made, Howard.

Having said that, if you would like to improve your vocabulary, I can tell you that you're going about it the right way by reading. Reading novels that use unfamiliar words is an excellent way to learn them because they're used correctly, in context. As Charles Harrington Elster said:

'For me, reading has always been not only a quest for pleasure and enlightenment but also a word-hunting expedition, a lexical safari.'

Having a large (considerable, extensive, substantial?) vocabulary means that you have the luxury of choice. Using the exact right word to describe something is very pleasing, both for the writer and the reader. Reading a sentence with sparkling vocabulary and quirky turns of phrase brings energy to the page. The opposite is also true: 'She took a moment to lament her lack of parasol. Every time she left the house, she felt keenly the absence of her heretofore ubiquitous accessory,' (Carol Garriger, *Timeless: Book 5 of The Parasol Protectorate*). It makes you smile at the pomposity of it, doesn't it? Where, outside a legal document, would you see the word 'heretofore'? (Although I see you used the word 'somewhat', which suggests a familiarity with more archaic terminology – well done).

Being comfortable with words and being able to play around with them does enhance

a story. In *Ulysses*, James Joyce uses 30,000 distinct words, that is, not repeated (rather than 'unrepeatable', but he uses a few of them too), but he also dared to create new ones and use existing words in new ways, such as making 'sausage' a verb and 'botch' a noun. I'm sure that you could apply these techniques yourself – you can still be inventive and imaginative using the vocabulary you have already.

The only risk I can see in enhancing your vocabulary is the danger of malapropisms, or using the wrong word. Originally coined by Richard Sheridan in his play *The Rivals*, Mrs Malaprop was famous for her errors, such as: 'I'm sorry to say, Sir Anthony, that my affluence over my niece is very small.' When used deliberately, malapropisms are great – a personal favourite of mine is saying 'I'm ravishing' rather than 'I'm ravenous' (which I first heard said by Ethel on *EastEnders*), but when it's an accident, it's painful.

So in answer to your letter, Gareth, immerse yourself in the world of words and take your pick of the ones you like – vocabulary is like seasoning, add a little to taste.

'Vocabulary is like seasoning, add a little to taste.'

Try this

» There are lots of online resources to increase your vocabulary, such as a word-a-day calendar, or signing up to receive a daily new word via email.

» The next time you spot a new word, add it to your own vocabulary by looking up the definition, writing it down and using it when you can. Turn it into a game by trying to use it in as many different conversations as possible.

» One way to give yourself a head start is by learning the root of words, often Greek or Latin. They can give you a clue as to the meaning as most words are built from common roots, prefixes and suffixes, for example 'ambi' means 'both' in Latin, which explains ambidextrous and ambiguous. It's also a fascinating glimpse into the original definition – as illustrated by Milan Kundera in *Ignorance*: 'The Greek word for "return" is nostos. Algos means "suffering." So nostalgia is the suffering caused by an unappeased yearning to return.'

Notes

Eleven
MY WRITING BORES ME

Carole, WHITNEY, OXON

I didn't find your letter boring. You used some great vocabulary; 'pedestrian' and 'lacklustre' are zingy words. I say this to point out something you may not have considered: that although *you* find your writing boring, don't assume that others will. Here at The Write Factor, the words of the poet John Moat are something of a motto to us:

'Your unique story is essential to the completion of the all-important universe story.'

You have got something to offer, even if you don't think you have. Have you considered showing your work to a friend? They may be able to reassure you.

But if I take you at your word, then there are lots of different approaches to add some zest to your writing. Even the most talented of writers can benefit from a good shake-up. That least-boring of artists, Andy Warhol suggested the best way to combat boredom is to:

'Let the little things that would ordinarily bore you suddenly thrill you.'

Deliberately choose to give yourself a new take on life. Choose a mundane activity such as the supermarket shop, and spice it up by only permitting yourself to buy things beginning with 'b'. Barolo and bratwurst, anyone? Or imagine the life of the person ahead of you in the queue, based on the contents of their shopping trolley. Or, how about deliberately getting lost in a place you are not familiar with: get on a tube, change stations, take a bus – see where you end up and how you get back. Who do you have to speak to? How did you feel? What did you see? Get outside your comfort zone; be playful.

The act of doing something out of the ordinary will trigger something in you and unleash a new confidence. The potential for new experiences and thus new material is limitless. All this new stimuli will get those neurons firing and hopefully add colour to your page. And whilst you're in the middle of nowhere, hopelessly lost, try eavesdropping on other people's conversations – it's a brilliant way to help you write convincing dialogue. Listen to how people engage with each other, write it down verbatim and then edit it to cut out the irrelevant or waffly sections.

If you're boring yourself, then it's time to look beyond your own experience. As writer Virginia Baily said:

'The process of writing is a leap into someone else's shoes. It is an act of empathy.'

Spend a day (metaphorically) in someone else's shoes. A paramedic for example. Do your research; find out what qualifications they need, what an average day might entail. Create a scenario – next door neighbour falls down the stairs – and you're the paramedic who attends the scene. What did you do? How did you feel? Do you love or hate your job? Do you have empathy with the patient, or do you have a desire to do them harm? What does it feel like to be in their skin? I'm assuming that you're not bored by other people – become one of them and inspire yourself.

Another idea is to return to your work (if you can bear to) and edit it. With a red pen, strike through any sentence that lacks oomph and rewrite it. Evie Wyld, author of *All the Birds, Singing*, has a beautifully creative turn of phrase, avoiding the obvious clichés. In place of 'it was windy' she says: 'The wind moved through the trees, down the chimney and into the front room where it waved through the top sheet of a newspaper.' Instead of, 'it got dark,' she writes: 'The light faded in waves, the tree branches became longer, hanging on to their shadows.' You can make your words work for you too, just by injecting them with a little quirkiness.

If your problem is that every story starts sounding the same, then you're stuck in a literary rut. Try writing in another 'voice' (a different genre, character or style): as I've mentioned previously, sometimes we can only find our voice after we've sounded like a lot of other people (to paraphrase the inspirational Neil Gaiman). So experiment: if you write romantic fiction, try writing a horror story; if you write in the first person, write in the third person; if you tend towards tragedy, try comedy. Surprise yourself.

The main thing to remember is that as a writer, you can play God. Your characters can do anything you tell them to, however extraordinary. You don't have to consider health and safety rules or social niceties – be as outrageous as you can. Here is the safest place to tell a lie. No *actual* consequences, no repercussions. Engaging the imagination is key to igniting your writing. Imagination isn't about fantasy worlds or magic and alchemy (although it is those things too), imagination is about alternatives. A friend who went to a drama workshop was instructed to improvise a scenario in which something disastrous happens. When he'd finished, he was then asked to make the situation worse, and repeat this until he had pushed it as far as he could. You need to approach your writing with the same attitude. Push it as far as it will go. Be extreme, be outrageous. Never mind that old adage:

Get those emotions out on the page and you'll never be boring again. As American playwright William Inge said: 'Nobody is bored when he is trying to make something that is beautiful, or to discover something that is true.'

'Write what you know', I say write what scares you.

Try this

» Practise making your words work harder for you by rewriting these sentences to make them sparkle:
  * The cat got stuck in the tree.
  * The woman tripped over.
  * I am hungry.
  * It was sunny.

» What happened to you today? What *might* have happened? Think of scenarios and imagine their alternatives. Imagine your life is a film set; describe it, embellish it, make the characters (your family) larger than life, heroes and villains, play God and make something incredible happen.

» Give yourself a workshop in sensory exploration. Instead of wolfing down your lunchtime sandwich in front of the computer, sit at the table and make yourself truly focus on it. How does it look? How does it taste? Does the taste change? Use all your senses to appreciate it and then write down your experience.

Notes

Twelve
I'LL NEVER BE FAMOUS

Mark, ST LEONARDS

That's quite a bleak letter, Mark. It makes me feel sad that you have become downhearted about writing and also furious that our society is so focused on success and celebrity that personal satisfaction has fallen by the wayside. Although I firmly believe there is a world more to writing than it being read (and will prove it to you shortly), I want to acknowledge this obsession with fame for a moment.

I'm interested in the idea that you *know* that you won't be famous. You sound so definite. What has lead you to this conclusion? Is it that you have sent your work off to agents and publishers and received nothing but rejections? Because they do sting. As Isaac Asimov said:

'Rejection slips, or form letters, however tactfully phrased, are lacerations of the soul, if not quite inventions of the devil - but there is no way around them.'

What I would take from this quote is not only the comfort of a fellow writer understanding the pain of work not being appreciated, but also the fact that it was written by, ahem, someone famous. Everybody has to start somewhere, even if it feels like you've been 'starting' for years.

Last year, JK Rowling tweeted her rejection letters she received when she was first writing under the pseudonym Robert Galbraith. She wanted aspiring authors to take comfort in the fact that her efforts were rejected out of hand. She was even advised to take a writing course by one (must be now mortified) agent. When she finally did get accepted, sales were modest. It was only when her secret identity was revealed that the book shot to the top of the bestseller's list. Joanne Harris (author of *Chocolat,* etc.) then commented on Rowling's tweet, saying that she received so many rejection letters that she made a sculpture of them. Which goes to show how fickle, how random, success is. And also how robust you need to be to continue writing, despite being rejected. You obviously feel that you have something to offer the world so I urge you not to give up sending off your manuscripts or entering competitions because there is someone out there who will appreciate your work.

Now to return to the subject mentioned earlier – does writing have any value if it doesn't reach a public platform? It's like the philosophical question about the tree falling in the forest – is a book any good if it's never been read? Of course, it's clear that you receive much ego-stroking when your work is read by many, but does that make it better than stories that never get to see the light of day? Is the point of writing for it to be read? I think not.

A funny and engaging blog post by Alex Mathers: *Four Killer Reasons Every Creative Person Must Write* hits the target dead on when he says about writing: 'It is not just for those who do it professionally and it's not only for those who want to write books. Writing has the power for us all to regain a hint of control amidst the chaos of reality.'

I like the idea of writing becoming a personal act of self-protection; that it helps carve out your own identity in an anonymous world.

Mathers also suggests that over and above the actual words on the page, there are benefits from just the act of writing, such as a form of therapy. 'When I put my thoughts to paper, I can feel the discharge of the energy that clings to them,' Mathers explains. He's right: writing has become a recognised therapeutic tool. A study by the University of Iowa found that writing about a traumatic experience helps the person deal with the emotions they experienced much more effectively than if they didn't, and it's particularly powerful if they describe the events as well as the feelings. So becoming the storyteller of your life helps you step away from the pain unhappy memories may evoke.

As well as emotional rewards, writing provides rational benefits too, as it helps to formulate ideas so you are able to communicate clearly. Mathers confesses to struggling with shyness, which makes talking to people difficult. He finds that he gets the message across much more succinctly and successfully via the written word. It also gives him the capacity to edit what he has written: 'The cool thing is you can read over what you write and order your words so that people think you're really clever.'

The ability to write (and you have this, regardless of what anyone says) is a sign of an interesting person with an inquiring mind. Using that ability keeps the flames of creativity lit, and it reminds you that you are more than just a: (fill in the blank) – wage-slave/father/son/partner. You have a skill that enhances your life and makes you use your mind for more than filling in sudokus. A pleasing turn of phrase, an evocative description, whatever you come up with is a sign that you are unique and important. Asking what is the point of writing is like asking what is the purpose of life. Only by doing it, by immersing yourself in it, will you discover the joy that it can bring.

'Writing has the power for us all to regain a hint of control amidst the chaos of reality.'

Try this

» Give yourself a boost by creating a blog – now you'll get to share your writing with the world, publisher or no publisher.

» Set up or join a writing group – hearing your work read aloud and receiving the praise of peers goes some way to fulfil that yearning for recognition.

» Imagine that you have published a book and it goes on to win the Man Booker Prize. What was this novel about? Try writing the opening sentence of it. Research has proven that if you mentally rehearse the goal you aim to achieve, you have a much better chance of making your fantasy a reality.

» If you ever question the purpose of writing again, remember this quote from Barack Obama: 'In my life, writing has been an important exercise to clarify what I believe, what I see, what I care about, what my deepest values are. The process of converting a jumble of thoughts into coherent sentences makes you ask tougher questions.'

Notes

Thirteen

AM I TOO OLD TO BE INTERESTING?

"I enjoy writing short stories and would love to win a competition but I worry that I'm being overlooked because I'm too old to be relevant. Are people interested in what a 76-year-old has to say?"

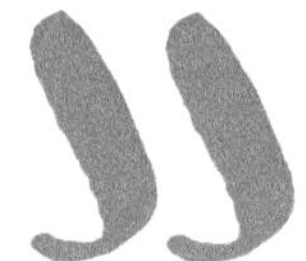

Michael, INVERNESS

I can see that you have been influenced by (and are suffering because of) the shift in perspective about age. Since the 1950s and the 'birth of the teenager', all the focus seems to be on youth; celebrating it, trying to cling on to it, even the phrase '40 is the new 30' suggests that there's something wrong with being 40. Well let me tell you now, Michael, any age is a great age to write.

It is a shame that a large sector of our society is now feeling overlooked, that their contribution is somehow considered lesser, not as vital, as younger people's. The stigma of old age is ridiculous, as no one can help getting older, it's just something that happens. As my colleague Lorna Howarth says: 'Modern society doesn't value the wisdom of the elders unlike more traditional cultures, where the elders are revered and their knowledge is held in high esteem. We would be wise to rekindle this respect, because a life well lived has many valuable lessons to impart. Currently, it takes courage to write when you are older precisely because our culture doesn't value us; we are consigned to the scrap-heap at retirement, and expected to sit quietly in care homes until our time comes to shuffle off this mortal coil.

It's time to say no thanks to that, and grasp the nettle of creative writing because it offers horizons that lead to the most interesting and unexpected of places. In later life, it is possible to recreate your life altogether by taking up the pen.'

A heartening article in *The Financial Times* recently detailed many great novelists who are prolific and successful well into their dotage: Philip Roth, Saul Bellow, Edna O'Brien, to name but a few. Wilbur Smith has just signed an eight-book deal at the age of 84 – eight years older than you. The journalist of this piece, Janan Ganesh, makes the interesting point that advances in medical science have lengthened our life expectancies, so that there is an increasing number of older people and consequently more demand for old novelists to reflect their experiences.

One of the great advantages of being older is that you (probably) have more time to devote to writing. The pressure is off to be the bread-winner/get that promotion/achieve those targets and you can spend time doing what you enjoy. What's more, one of the unexpected bonuses of feeling overlooked and insignificant is that it gives you licence to do what you want. As Lorna continues: 'We have been working with an older writer who is becoming more prolific as time goes by, because he feels he has more to say about life and he chooses to do this via fiction, to really free him up from the restrictions of memoir-writing. Very often, memoirs can implicate family members – Chrissie Hynde once said that she couldn't write her memoir until her parents had died – and he finds that only by writing fiction can he tell the truth, which is an interesting paradox in itself.'

Take Chrissie Hynde's lead and see your situation as an opportunity to go wild. Either you can spill the beans about long-dead relatives who aren't around to be offended, or you can use the framework of a memoir but subvert the facts. How about writing about the career/relationship/family you wished you'd had? What would have happened if you'd taken a different path at a particular crossroads in your life? This is the opportunity to explore a parallel dimension; the life you lived where whatever you hoped for, happened. You can make dreams come true (on the page, of course).

As well as these flights of fancy, you could also explore the reality of being in your seventies. You assume that this is not 'relevant' or of interest to readers but that very much depends on how it is written. Lorna's client writes perceptively and with breathtaking honesty about life after the loss of a life partner, and the repercussions of starting again in one's seventies. It is a subject that will resonate with many readers and perhaps encourage them to write about their own experiences, which can be incredibly cathartic.

A famous example of writing in later life is that of Mary Wesley, who wrote her most successful books – *The Chamomile Lawn* amongst them – in her seventies. It wasn't just a case of having the time to write in her later years, but that as time goes by, there is a nostalgia about and hunger for information about certain periods of history. Mary Wesley wrote about life during the war, but older people could just as well write about their experience of, for example, life in the swinging sixties, or life in the aftermath of a natural disaster.

What event in your life resonates most with you? You can be sure that is the subject that will most fascinate the reader, as the emotions of the time naturally embed themselves among the recollections. I have noticed as a creative writing tutor that the students' pieces based on personal experience are often much more convincing and expressive than pure fiction, simply because they're perfect vignettes ready to transfer from memory to page, rather than via the laborious process of making them up.

I'm sorry that your confidence has suffered a blow but please be reassured that you still have plenty to offer. As the FT writer beautifully put it (about older writers):

'These are not people easing into eternity like the benign grandfather in the Werther's Original ad. There is a force to their writing that the young cannot buy, surely caused, not eased, by awareness of the ultimate deadline.'

Try this

» Don't be limited by what it says on your birth certificate – write a piece from the perspective of each decade of your life – starting as a ten-year-old. Then enter your best story into a Writers' Forum competition!

» Prove that hackneyed adage 'age is just a number' to be true and challenge yourself to do something typically targeted towards a younger generation: surfing, vlogging, going to a music festival and then write about it. Describe how it felt – liberating, revitalising or embarrassing?

» Francis Bacon can't be wrong: 'Age appears to be best in four things; old wood best to burn, old wine to drink, old friends to trust and old authors to read.

Notes

Fourteen
HOW WEIRD IS TOO WEIRD?

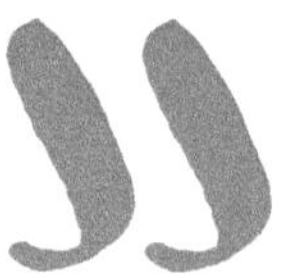

Gina, READING

I'm intrigued, Gina – just how weird are you thinking? Is it as weird as *Alphabetical Africa?* This book by Walter Abish begins by only allowing words starting with 'a' in the first chapter, then including 'b' words in the second and so on. (First line: *Ages ago, Alex, Allen and Alva arrived at Antibes, and Alva allowing all, allowing anyone, against Alex's admonition, against Allen's angry assertion: another African amusement.)*

Or perhaps you were thinking more along the lines of James Joyce's famously inaccessible *Finnegan's Wake* – the book everyone's heard of and no-one's finished reading. (Sample line: *What then agentlike brought about that tragoady thundersday this municipal sin business? Our cubehouse still rocks as earwitness to the thunder of his arafatas...)* The spellcheck on my computer is going crazy, with red underlines a-go-go, just transcribing this.

Both these books earn a tick in the 'weird' box and both have been published, proving that it's possible to be successfully weird. Their weirdness, the difference that stands them apart from others, is celebrated. I understand your hesitance though. There is a very fine line between being weird and being unreadable. You certainly don't want your readers to snap your book shut with a huff of irritation, you want to bewitch and mesmerise them.

One book currently on my bedside cabinet is *City of Circles* by Jess Richards. This story, about a tight-rope walker, funnily enough, certainly walks that line and I must admit this is why I haven't finished it yet. Sometimes it tips just a little too far into weird for my liking. Magical realism doesn't really float my boat and this book has it in spades. In one section the central character, Danu, sets up home in a derelict house, but the house (Number 19) objects and tries to eject her. 'Number 19 is a touch irritated and more than a little intrigued. For a long time it has wanted to fully understand how human atmospheres work.'

It's all too much for me, so I stopped halfway and switched to the far more conventional *Us* by David Nichols. However, I know someone who has a lot more time (and patience) for magic realism and will definitely appreciate *City of Circles*: my colleague Lorna Howarth who loves the stories of Gabriel Garcia Marquez and Yann Martell, whose books some think are a bit 'out there'. The point to be gleaned from this is that whilst some may be put off by more esoteric writing, others lap it up. It's true that you may antagonise some potential readers, but you may charm and beguile others. There's nothing to be gained from trying to please everyone and ending up too bland and compromised to please anyone.

The central core to your letter is about risk. Is it worth taking a risk? Because a risk means the chance of failure. And I say yes. If the gamble pays off, then you're a winner. The master of taking risks is Samuel Beckett. Who else would write a whole play with just one character wallowing in mud? Here's a glimpse of Beckett's particular brand of weird in *How It Is*: 'The tongue gets clogged with mud that can happen too only one remedy then pull it in and suck it swallow the mud or spit it out it's one or the other and question is it nourishing and vistas last a moment with that.'

One of the most effective ways to explore weirdness is to contrast it with normality. An incredibly moving account by someone who has explored both the rational and the mysterious side of existence first hand is Dr Jill Bolte Taylor. In an inspiring TEDtalk she shares what it was like to have a stroke from the perspective of a neuroscientist. As the left side of her brain ceased to function, the methodical thought processes residing here that kept her tethered to 'normal thinking' stopped and she became aware of a sense of being connected to the universe. 'Because I could not identify the position of my body in space, I felt enormous and expansive, like a genie just liberated from her bottle. And my spirit soared free like a great whale gliding through the sea of silent euphoria. Harmonic. I remember thinking there's no way I would ever be able to squeeze the enormousness of myself back inside this tiny little body.'

As this articulate and academic scientist describes this epiphany, tears course down her cheeks unchecked. She is unashamed about venturing far 'off-piste' in conceptual terms, far, far away from her scientific comfort zone and ecstatic about what she discovered there. I watched this TEDtalk a few years ago but I still think about it and regularly implore people to watch it (including you). It had a massive impact on me; her unflinchingly accurate and precise description of being desperately ill, the juxtaposition between the nerdy brainbox and the life-changing cosmic exploration she had and most of all her honesty. Her talk is sending the message: 'Something weird but important happened to me, I want to tell you all about it.'

This mentality is something we should all aim for. We should chuck out self-doubt, jettison worries of being too unconventional and bring something so fresh and unique to the table that readers, publishers, editors, cannot tear themselves away from it.

'Dare to be different and when you do this, you will be rewarded with the highest accolade – being memorable.'

Try this

- » Bring out the inner weirdo by first identifying what's in your literary comfort zone. Look at where you are happiest and choose the polar opposite – so if you like writing historical bodice rippers, write a sci-fi poem.

- » Make your tale unexpected by going against your instincts, for example if you have created a likeable character, experiment with killing her off or if you gravitate towards happy endings, write a tragedy.

- » For a fantastic example of taking a literary risk, read Seamus Deane's *Reading in the Dark*, where the story is told by a boy hiding under the table. The reader only learns that the boy's dying sister is being taken to hospital by the glimpses of adult feet that he sees.

Notes

Fifteen

IS ONE SORT OF WRITING BETTER THAN ANOTHER?

Laura, HAMBLE

I can't wait for your book to be published, Laura. There is nothing more enjoyable than reading a really good chick-lit book that addresses all the issues that I face in day-to-day life – friendships, parenting and so on. The only problem I have with it is the name: 'chick-lit.' It's so dismissive, so withering. The queen of the chick-lit genre herself, Marian Keyes, seller of over 30 million books, said as much to The Hay Festival last year [2015]: 'It's definitely a pejorative term. I'm going to quote Gandhi here: "First they ignore you, then they mock you, then they fight you," This is very much a patriarchal society. And I think one way of keeping women less well paid and having to do more work is to mock them and anything they love. And I'm not saying this in anger – it's a simple fact that one way of keeping women shut up is to call the things they love "fluff". It's a device.'

I think that's true. There is a huge snobbery in literary circles that achieves nothing apart from making a (self-nominated) chosen few feel superior and the rest of us feel inferior, as you have realised. It's effectively squashing certain voices because they don't fit in with a perceived notion of 'highbrow'. In a great piece in *The New York Times*, writer Pankaj Mishra said:

'Such distinctions as lowbrow, highbrow and middlebrow are now mostly useful in identifying their early adopters: a tiny minority of artists and intellectuals who felt a sense of siege as capitalism became global.'

So being highbrow only matters to those who are.

Your chosen genre of writing may not be as esteemed or as lofty as some, but it is still an incredible achievement, not to be minimised by comparison to other genres. My colleague, Lorna Howarth, has been working with novelist Casey O'Connor, producing her first novel: *Being Bridie.* It could certainly be described as chick lit, but Casey is very proud of it. 'It is the most incredible thing I've done in my life. When I tell people I've written a book they look at me differently,' she said. I don't think people stop to ask what genre it is first before they're impressed, Laura. Writing is writing, and a monumental effort, to be congratulated.

Lorna has also observed that the practise of writing in itself has huge value:

'The writing process is perhaps more important than who's going to read it. If you're telling your story, enjoying it and it gives you confidence, that in itself is reason enough to write it.'

Our work at The Write Factor is as much about the author and the process as it is about the finished product.

You know how hard it is to write, so don't undervalue your work by judging it against some arbitrary notion of high art. However, I think it's important to address your point that some books are seen as more important than others, and to perhaps understand why this is. The word 'highbrow' derives from the Victorian craze for phrenology – gauging someone's intelligence by the shape of their skull – so literally a high brow means having a bigger brain, thus more intelligence. A 'clever' book is therefore deemed more impressive because it's assumed you have to be clever to appreciate it.

In an insightful article on the Kill Your Darlings (great quote there!) website, writer Hannah Kent argues that because 'lowbrow' literature is easier to read and less challenging, it's

merely entertainment rather than insightful or inspiring. She likens it to a pony-ride at a fair and says: 'Highbrow literature is different. Highbrow literature is a bareback gallop in the wilderness. At night... There's no one to hold your hand. It's not sanitised. It requires something of you. Highbrow books might not flatter you or cater to your ego, but you know that bareback horse is taking you somewhere.'

She sees highbrow literature as more enriching, and therefore more important. Kent also cites the fact that Iranian author and professor, Azar Nafisi used to share forbidden classic novels with female students as a way of empowering them and that there was a reason he chose Nabokov over Dan Brown. She ends her piece with this: 'Dear reader, if you had to choose between burning the highbrow books and destroying them forever, or setting fire to the lowbrow books, which pile would you set your match to? I rest my case.'

It's clear where her priorities lie, but why have an ultimatum? Can't both exist in the world and be equally revered, for different reasons? I'm reminded of what my old editor at *Take a Break* (very lowbrow!) magazine used to say: 'We're not in the business of educating people, we want to entertain,' and that was the central tenet of the magazine. My point is that there is nothing wrong with being entertained. In fact, it's one of the greatest things in life. I'm sure Hannah Kent would put Shakespeare in the highbrow camp, yet some of his humour is decidedly lavatorial (calling a character 'Bottom', anyone?)

Shakespeare managed to be influential, ground-breaking and inspiring whilst also being (at times) light-hearted and playful. He didn't feel constrained by the pressure of being highbrow all the time and also saw the value of levity. Be like Shakespeare, Laura. Don't feel that just because your work probably falls under the label of chick-lit that it can't also contain insights and wisdom that will enlighten as well as entertain.

In all areas of the arts, lines are being blurred between 'intellectual' and 'non-intellectual' pursuits – Roy Lichtenstein and Andy Warhol played with ideas of what was 'art' by using cartoons and soup tins in their work, smashing boundaries to prepare the ground for the artists who followed them. David Hockney was one of the first artists to incorporate words into paintings, making people question their preconceived notions of what is acceptable. Neil Gaiman is another who dares to flout convention, bringing respectability to comics, sorry, 'graphic novels'.

Just as there is room in the world for both high and lowbrow literature, so there is room within your work for both thought-provoking concepts whilst being an 'easy read'. Don't see chick-lit as a limitation, see it as a great foundation from which to explore your potential as a writer.

Try this

- » Read widely to get an idea of how others break down the boundaries between genres – there are lots of books out there that are cracking good page-turners but also fresh, challenging and original, such as *The Rose Project* or *Me Before You*.

- » Take heart with what **Anuradha Bhattacharyya** says: 'School children, who have enjoyed reading a romance or a detective thriller or a novel about terror and conquest, make the invariable mistake of studying literature in college. They make the mistake of learning theory in place of art; they acquire impediments in their own enjoyment of the books by allowing a set of theories to govern their own reading.'

Notes

Sixteen
WRITING A TEAR-JERKER

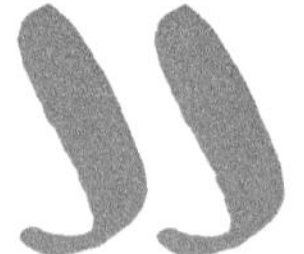

Jo, ALTRINCHAM

I love a good weepie too, so I applaud your efforts. It's curious as to why we actively seek out things that make us cry, as you'd think that we'd want to avoid this particular emotion. Whilst researching the answer for your question, Jo, I found myself at the mercy of one of those irresistible 'click-bait' adverts for websites that lure you in with a challenge. This particular one was: 'Can you make it through this post without crying?' (Google 'Buzzfeed' and the challenge title if you want to try it yourself.) And what followed was a series of heart-warming photos and poignant stories. As a hardened journalist, I thought this would be easy to resist. Very little makes me sniff. But sure enough, by the end, I found myself welling-up, and what did it? A picture of Kermit the frog, of all the absurd things. The reason it tugged at my heartstrings was because it was of him looking up at a picture of Jim Henson, the Muppets creator, who had died.

Afterwards, I didn't feel annoyed or ashamed, I felt filled with empathy for humanity and the suffering we go through, and yes, that includes Kermit the frog. So although it seems counter-intuitive to seek out sadness, it's understandable because crying over something we read or watch serves three purposes, psychologically. Firstly, it's a safe outlet to release pent-up emotions – tears contain stress hormones, and as we cry we literally (yes, literally, not figuratively!) reduce the levels of these hormones. Secondly, we get a feel-good buzz from the compassion we feel for the characters; we're crying because we care about them, and caring makes us feel all warm and fuzzy. Finally, as we watch our characters go through the mill, it makes us reflect on our own circumstances and feel relieved that we're doing okay, comparatively. We think: 'My life may not be perfect but at least I haven't been wrongfully accused of rape,' and sniff happily as we continue to read *Atonement*.

So hoping to write a tear-jerker is a laudable pursuit. You're right that the term 'tear-jerker' is particularly abrasive. I think it comes from the fact that people feel scornful about the way emotions can be deliberately manipulated to create an emotional scene. The negative connotations are also due to the risk of being mawkish or overly sentimental. But:

Ian McEwan has never been accused of being mawkish, and *Atonement* definitely makes you cry.

One of the key points is to not over-egg the pudding. Gushy, purple prose will only induce nausea, instead of sadness. A recent student on The Write Factor's Absolute Beginner's course wrote a beautiful but heart-wrenching short story and managed to avoid any sentimentality by simply letting the situation play out naturally. The moment when the central character learns that her unborn baby has died in the womb is handled so sensitively and delicately. She skilfully chooses to have the fact delivered by a doctor, and his calm demeanour is a wonderful counterpoint to the highly charged moment. "'I am afraid there is no heartbeat. Your baby has died. You see here," he points at my child's skull on the screen and clicks the mouse, "here you see there is a crossing over of the skull plates," he moves around the little arrows and dots on the picture. "This happens when your baby dies.'"

A great example of less is more. High drama, enormous tragedy, so plainly expressed that the reader has room to think for themselves instead of having their nose squashed right up against it. If the scene were to be written from the mother's point of view, there would be a danger of veering into maudlin waters and it being over the top. Taking a step back and providing another point of view is a great technique when handling high drama. It also frames the moment elegantly, allowing the information to sink in. There is also the benefit of providing another witness to the moment, which increases the main character's heroism. She is going through hell but is also stoical and controlled in the clinical setting.

Having a slightly detached approach also flatters the reader because it enables them to provide their own interpretation of events, which is why you often hear about the importance of 'show not tell' in writing. This understatement is employed well in the book: *Hiroshima* by Pulitzer prize-winning author John Hersey. An extremely dark subject matter, made palatable, engaging, readable, by presenting the facts without over-dramatisation.

Another technique to encourage pathos is to keep hope alive within your writing, even if it is unrealistic. You build up the readers' expectations to make them continue reading and then dash them. For example, if you include a diagnosis of cancer, you don't reveal that it's terminal until the end so that there's always the chance our hero/heroine will survive. The brilliant book *Being Dead* by John Crace is a great example of how the reverse is true – Crace ensures that we know from the beginning (or even before that, from the title) that the couple have been murdered, and as a result you don't feel remotely sad about it but you do care about them.

You could also try making your characters be in denial about their situation, to increase the poignancy. For example, a child with a terminal illness saying: 'I'm not going to die, am I, Mummy?' produces a lump in your throat because the optimism in the face of reality is so touching.

Above all, the most important thing to remember when writing a weepie, is something that's true for all writing, sad or not: the reader must care about the characters. This can only be achieved by effective, realistic description. If you have described someone so vividly that it's impossible not to care when disaster strikes for them, then your work is done. Throw yourself into your writing and write from the heart, with sincerity and integrity. Then your reader won't think: 'that's sad' but: 'I can't help but cry.'

Try this

» Don't be too flowery; keep the descriptions and dialogue simple and clear, and avoid melodrama or cliché.

» Try this writing exercise: Remember a time of great sadness in your own life and instead of trying to describe it in the first person, write it as if you were an impartial bystander, recording how you looked, sounded and acted. Try to include realistic observations to make it even more convincing.

» Get philosophical – move away from the high drama and bring an element of reflection into the piece to make the reader think about life's big issues.

Notes

Seventeen
I'M SELF-CONSCIOUS ABOUT MY WRITING

"How do I cope with the fact that I find being a writer slightly embarrassing? I enjoy writing but the whole process – 'finding your voice', 'writing from the heart', is cringe-worthy. I also find talking about writing makes me sound pompous and I feel terribly self-conscious. Should I just get over myself?"

Simon, SALTAIRE

I love your letter, Simon as you've really hit the nail on the head about some aspects of being a writer. Even the phrase: 'I'm a writer' conjures up an image of a salon of word-smiths archly exchanging pithy *bon mots* à la Dorothy Parker. What is it exactly that makes this scenario so excruciating? Is it the lack of awareness of how self-absorbed they are? Is it the assumption of superiority over mere laypeople who don't have a 'simply darling' turn of phrase to hand? Or could it be that, at heart, it touches that nerve that we all have – the fear of failure and of opening yourself up to criticism? Is that the reason that you feel ambivalent about writing and the image it has, making you want to distance yourself from being associated with it?

If you said: 'I'm a doctor' you could expect a much simpler reaction, one of admiration and respect, but swap that career for writing and the (anticipated) response is much more complex. It involves preconceptions and prompts follow-on questions such as how successful you are, whether you have written anything they've heard of and fundamentally, *are you any good?* Because writing is so personal, an intimate expression of how you feel about the world, you are opening your-self up to criticism and scrutiny in a way that you aren't if you have a more straightforward career or hobby.

There are lots of emotions swirling around here relating to making yourself vulnerable, wanting to express yourself and self-doubt, so let's start at the beginning and try to unpack them. First of all, it's a good sign that you enjoy writing. Hold on to that because it's very precious. You don't have to win the Man Booker Prize, you don't have to ever show your work to anyone, but if the act of putting pen to paper gives you pleasure, that's reason enough to keep on doing it.

However, the fact that you've written to me suggests that your discomfort is something you'd like to come to terms with, to be able to share your work and talk about it without feeling foolish. My colleague, Lorna Howarth, remembers how embarrassment used to dog her during her early career: 'When I was first working at *Resurgence* magazine, when my articles were published I couldn't even look at them. I felt a flood of adrenalin run through my body as the magazines were delivered to the office. It was almost the 'flight or fight' reaction, because I was ultimately responsible for my article. Despite the fact that it had been sub-edited and passed by the editor-in-chief, I questioned my ability to write: What if I got some facts wrong? What if it's badly written? What if people disagree and we get loads of letters to the editor saying I'm useless? None of these things came to pass, but it took me quite a while to own my writing without being embarrassed by it.'

'It took me quite a while to own my writing without being embarrassed by it.'

Happily, for Lorna the embarrassment wasn't enough to stop her writing, and so it shouldn't be for you, Simon. As JRR Tolkien said: 'A man that flies from his fear may find that he has only taken a short cut to meet it.' Don't sacrifice writing because some elements mortify you, rather, dig down to what the problem is and overcome it. Remember, the risk of embarrassment is worth the reward of other people enjoying your work.

Lorna recognised that she could tolerate having her work in print when she acknowledged that her take on the world was equally as valid as anyone else's and suggests that you do the same. 'You have a right to express your views but you have to also 'man-up' because just like in real life, some people are bound to disagree with you or will not like what you're saying which they may express in reviews and criticism. Any bad review is enough to make you want to go and hide under a stone, but ultimately, if you like your writing and you're proud of it and can stand by it, then so be it. Everyone else is entitled to their opinions too. It's about owning your work and accepting that nobody is infallible.'

There *is* an element of embarrassment in revealing your thoughts without hiding behind sarcasm or cynicism and it's something you have to learn to tolerate. Just like when someone asks you how you are, and you answer truthfully and in detail, including bunions, rashes and insomnia, it's shocking to write something brutally honest and unflinching. When you read a passage filled with searing emotion in context, it's amazing, but if it's examined in the cold light of day, it can make your toes curl. It's this juxtaposition of the realities of day-to-day life and the passion and honesty that writing requires that is difficult to juggle but perhaps being aware of it will lessen the pain. Why not unpick the emotion of embarrassment and write about it? *Blott on the Landscape* by Tom Sharpe feasts and delights on this feeling, to great effect.

To address the second emotion – the desire to express yourself – there is no point being bland and anodyne in your writing to lessen the response it invokes, because you'll only succeed in being boring.

You must push yourself to the limit, to explore the darkest, highest and most painful emotions to write effectively.

Finally, the particular practises such as writing from the heart, finding your voice and writing a stream of consciousness all require you to plunge in without scrutiny and self-criticism. If it's the particular way these ideas are phrased that gets to you, rephrase them into something more acceptable, using a technique such as 'free writing' (where you write without judgement or self-censorship). Ignore the voice in your head telling you that these techniques are somehow indulgent and leave you open to ridicule – it's the same voice that wants to squash any creativity. Dare to take risks and revel in the results.

Try this

- » Bear in mind what CS Lewis said: 'Even in social life, you will never make a good impression on other people until you stop thinking about what sort of impression you're making.'

- » You find writing embarrassing? So write your most embarrassing moment and show it to someone. Feel the fear and do it anyway, to quote a certain self-help book.

- » Reward yourself for conquering your embarrassment with a favourite treat. Too often we berate ourselves for our perceived failings rather than celebrating our successes.

Notes

Eighteen
HOW CAN I BE FUNNY?

"My dream is to write a comedy but my efforts don't even raise a chortle. Am I destined to always write serious prose or is there some way I can give my work an injection of humour?"

Esther, STAMFORD

Thank you for your letter, Esther. Researching my response has been great fun. I can understand why you would like to write comedy as it's such a rewarding genre, not only for the writer but for the reader too. We're born with an inherent desire to laugh – it explains why we endlessly scroll through social media sites in search of one more chuckle. Laughter is a powerful tool in society – it serves two functions: to help us bond with our social group and to lessen anxiety and tension. It gives us a break from our humdrum lives, or even just puts a comic spin on them, and the people who can make us laugh are much admired.

I remember reading *Adrian Mole aged 13¾* when it first came out, and what stayed with me more than the book itself was the puff quote on the front cover by Tom Sharpe:

'I not only wept, I howled and hooted and had to get up and walk around the room and wipe my eyes so that I could go on reading.'

Isn't that a dream compliment? A famous (and very funny) author literally crying with laughter at your work. But this needn't remain a fantasy – it is possible to learn to write comedy. The great thing about it – indeed about writing itself – is that it's egalitarian. The likes of Sue Townsend are good at it, but then people all around you are too – from amusing comments on Facebook to the shop assistant with a ticklish outlook on life. The tricky bit is translating these comic moments into prose.

It can help to understand *why* something is funny. A rich seam of comedy gold can be found in the bizarre – something so unexpected and incongruent that it's hilarious.

In an article in *The Independent*, Graham Linehan (writer of *Father Ted, Black Books* and *The IT Crowd*) said: 'To borrow an image from David Lynch, you're looking for the big fish. The tiddlers flashing about just below the surface – the trite observations, the easy targets, the established joke-constructions – you need to ignore them and wait for the big one: an image or scene that makes you double over with laughter and could only have come from deep within your subconscious. To give you an example from my own work, Mrs Doyle, wondering where the "perfectly square bit of black dirt" on the window came from is a set-up so odd the audience doesn't even think of it as a set-up, and enjoys it for its own sake. So when Ted appears at the window with a Hitler moustache (and that's the big fish, that's what Arthur Mathews and I thought of first), one of the reasons it works is that the audience didn't realise we were setting them up.'

To introduce the element of surprise, like Graham Linehan, you need to set the scene and then confound expectations by leading the reader somewhere they don't expect to go. For example you could say:

'Esther was a healthy eater, she loved everything green, especially mint choc-chip ice cream.'

This is funny because the punchline is unexpected. Similarly, Alan Bennett's one-liner: 'I'm all in favour of free expression provided it's kept rigidly under control,' also makes us do a mental double-take.

Another enjoyable comedic avenue is double-entendre – 'Esther enjoyed camping, there was nothing more she liked than opening her flaps in the morning.' If this is a bit too 'Carry On' for you then you can also have a lot of fun with the words themselves. To return to comedy royalty, Alan Bennett is the master of the beautifully turned phrase that is so familiar, so mundane that it's genius, artfully illustrated in his series of monologues, *Talking Heads*.

'If Jesus were alive today Mrs Whittaker, I think you'd find these were the type of shoes he'd be wearing' – Alan Bennett

Victoria Wood was also a queen at exquisitely observed humour written in such intricate sentences that they take your breath away. From her TV series: 'I've just had my TV mended. I say mended – a shifty young man in plimsolls waggled my aerial and wolfed my Gipsy Creams but that's the comprehensive system for you.' This is peppered with so many comedy devices, from the word 'waggled' to the mention of Gipsy Creams that we're left gasping. Swapping a generic for a specific brand is sure-fire success – an apricot Nissan Micra conjures up a more vivid image than an orange car. My six-year-old daughter makes me laugh when she uses the number 152 to describe things, such as, 'There must be 152 snails in the strawberry patch' – much funnier than just saying 'hundreds'.

If you hear something that amuses you, jot it down, it may be a turn of phrase, an observation or even just a word. Many writers go back over their work, substituting words which they deem funnier. Much analysis has gone into why some words are funnier than others – some have suggested that the 'k' sound is inherently funny, so saying 'chicken' is funnier than 'hen', 'sprinkle' rather than pour. Also, some words are funny because they sound unusual, such as 'waddle', 'snuffle', 'canoodle' and 'gumption'.

Also, examine the pace of your sentences. Changing the pace and rhythm can be funny, for example:

'His favourite places to go were the Taj Mahal, the Leaning Tower of Pisa and Asda.'

This device can also be used in varying syllables, such as: 'She had three brothers: Sebastian, Montgomery and Bob.'

In essence, comedy is about being aware of the rules and then breaking them. Anything can be comedic fodder, even the darkest of subjects.

In his memoir, *Cancer on $5 a Day* (*Chemo Not Included)* Robert Schimmel manages to make cancer funny: 'This stupid hospital gown is riding up my ass. I try to pull it down and it snaps right back up like a window shade. I cross my legs and suddenly I'm Sharon Stone.'

So, return to your work, Esther, and use these methods to add some laughs. The great thing about comedy writing is that it's not just the end result that matters, but also that you'll have fun trying.

Try this

» Try this exercise on incongruence. Write down 'who', 'what', 'when', 'where' and 'why' across a sheet of paper. Then choose a situation, such as a summer fair. Now think up the most unlikely characters, places and motives – it's the opposite of free association: what *don't* you associate with a summer fair? Unusual and hopefully funny scenarios will present themselves to you, such as setting it in the arctic with World War One soldiers.

» To hone your word-selection skills, find the funniest word to end these sentences:
    * Esther knew she was happiest in the _________
    * Paul opened the parcel and inside was a __________
    * After an exhausting 12-hour climb to the summit, everyone treated themselves to a _______

» Start with a tired simile and change it for comic effect, for example: 'It's as easy as pie' is boring – how could it be made funny? Perhaps: 'It's as easy as spilling red wine on a cream carpet' or 'overeating at Christmas'?

Notes

Nineteen
ORIGINAL THINKING

"How can I be more original? Everything I write seems to be derivative. With the thousands of books already out there, is it even possible to write something new and fresh?"

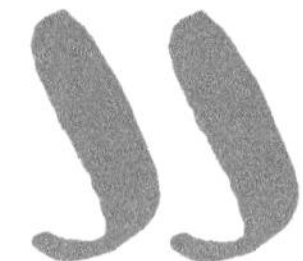

Maxine, GLASTONBURY

The holy grail of writing, Maxine, originality. Wouldn't it be great if every word we wrote was so startlingly different, unique and challenging that readers fell off their chairs with surprise, mid-sentence? It's a noble aim, indeed, but somewhat hard to achieve, or at least, to sustain.

Controversially, KM Weiland, author and mentor says that originality is unimportant: 'Most readers love experiencing the same story over and over again. The same goes for authors. Often, we harvest our initial kernel of inspiration from the work of another author whose story we love.'

As King Solomon said: 'There's nothing new under the sun,' so don't be disheartened by your attempts to be original.

This doesn't mean to say, however, that a new take on a familiar story can't be original. They do say that there are only seven plotlines – as defined in Christopher Booker's *The Seven Basic Plots* (somewhat ironically described as,

'breathtaking in its scope and *originality*' by the publisher!):

* overcoming the monster
* rags to riches
* the quest
* voyage and return
* comedy
* tragedy
* rebirth

These plots form the skeletons that can be fleshed out with new versions of the same story. They may have the same narrative arc but they can be as different as *Cinderella* and *The Wolf of Wall Street*. Both are rags to riches stories but are in no way similar, apart from the premise.

Dorothy L Sayers puts it succinctly: 'The amount of matter in the universe is limited… But no such limitation of numbers applies to the creation of works of art. The poet is not obliged, as it were, to destroy the material of *Hamlet* in order to create a Falstaff, as a carpenter must destroy a tree-form to create a table-form. The components of the material world are fixed; those of the world of imagination increase by a continuous and irreversible process, without any destruction or rearrangement of what went before.'

The use of the word: 'Imagination' here is crucial. In your imagination, Maxine, the possibilities are endless. The breathtakingly funny, shocking and fresh BBC Three drama *Fleabag*, by Phoebe Waller-Bridge was developed when the writer started with events that had happened to her and then ran with them, fantasising about what could have happened next. So they didn't emerge, fully-formed, from her keyboard, but are based on events in her life, mixed with flights of fancy.

Look at pivotal events in your life and take them as a source of inspiration. We all go through roughly the same daily life – wake up, eat, do stuff, sleep – but the different permutations of this is what makes it fascinating. You had breakfast this morning, but what are the little differences that makes that interesting to someone else? Perhaps you're Japanese and had rice and fish? Perhaps you're a shift worker and your 'morning' starts at 10 in the evening? This reminds me of the brilliant scene in *Pulp Fiction*, where Vince tells Jules that in France they call a Big Mac, 'Le Big Mac'. It's a lovely observation and just one reason why Quentin Tarantino's dialogue often feels so convincing. Chain restaurants are known and loved for their predictability and uniformity, and spotting this difference brings a fresh interpretation of a familiar experience.

Your own personal version of the world is what makes your story original.

The second point about *Fleabag* is that it's also part of a brand of risk-taking, female-centred comedy such as *Bridesmaids* and *Girls* that is currently breaking the mould. Could Waller-Bridge have written it without these forerunners? We shall never know, but there's certainly nothing wrong with being in a certain bracket, being compared to high-quality writing that's gone before. Our frame of reference is built-up from thousands, if not millions, of different influences that all go together towards creating our own personal view of the world. We bring this to our writing too. KM Weiland uses the interesting analogy of a bubble: 'Readers and authors alike are content to live within that bubble of un-originality for a while. But then the trends begin to evolve. They start pushing at the walls of the bubble, poking, prodding, and expanding, until suddenly they burst through and something new and exciting rolls forth – and creates a new bubble within which everyone's stories live for a while before the cycle repeats.'

A good example of something that's burst KM Weiland's bubble is the original and hugely enjoyable drama series *Black Mirror,* by Charlie Brooker. He pushes the boundaries, taking our traditional preconceptions and pushing them to the nth degree to create a frightening dystopia. You can see how he generates his ideas though. He systematically examines the obsessions of the 21st century – Facebook, mobile phones, computer games, the power of the media and so on, and then asks: 'what if...?' 'How could this go wrong?', 'what is one of the possible nightmare conclusions to this?' So his originality is rooted in the subversion of existing forms. You can apply this to your own work. We expect a certain order in our lives, creating a comfort zone around us when we keep within these limitations. Dare to go outside your comfort zone, see what happens if your central character dies mid-sentence, for example.

Whilst you're in this exciting, unpredictable landscape, start to question everything you've taken as read. Rip-up your rulebook and start afresh. Have an opinion on the world around you and make it shocking. I love Kurt Vonnegut's vitriolic take on harmless semi-colons, describing them as 'transvestite hermaphrodites representing absolutely nothing.' You may not agree; if you don't, then write the opposing line, making it just as colourful. Double-check your reflexive instinct in your writing and allow new thoughts to emerge.

Searching for original ideas is like panning for gold – generally non-productive but occasionally you come up with a nugget of genius.

And the rest of the time – just rework and re-examine what's left to make it unique to you.

Try this

» Practice bringing your own slant to the world by choosing a thought-provoking picture and describing what's going on in it. Who is the hero? What has just happened? Bring the picture to life and make it part of a narrative.

» If challenging yourself with your ideas is not working, imagine you're writing for someone you know. What would they find interesting/ funny/fresh?

» Take one of the characters you've written about before and make them the complete opposite. Dare to shock with how different they are: if you have a cosy grandma, keep her as such, but make her transgender/a surfer/an insomniac. Why not?

Notes

Twenty
I DON'T ENJOY WRITING

"I am writing to you with a curious problem in that the answer to it seems plain, but it isn't to me. My problem is that I don't enjoy writing. You would think that the solution would be simply not to do it, but then I would feel as if I have let something that is important to me go. What should I do?"

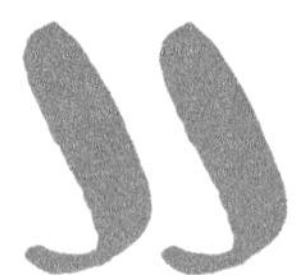

Emma, FISHGUARD

A thorny conundrum if ever there was one, Emma, and one that I can relate to. Without wanting to steal your thunder, this is a battle that I have struggled with all my (writing) life, so I completely understand the difficult place you find yourself in. You can see that you have a talent for writing and perhaps also have something to offer but the actual process throws up many psychological barriers so it becomes unpleasant; a chore. You end up asking yourself, what is the point of doing something that you don't find enjoyable.

Novelist Hari Kunzru described the writing process vividly: 'there are the pitfalls of self-disgust, boredom, disorientation and a lingering sense of inadequacy, occasionally alternating with episodes of hysterical self-congratulation as you fleetingly believe you've nailed that particular sentence and are surely destined to join the ranks of the immortals, only to be confronted the next morning with an appalling farrago of clichés that no sane human could read without vomiting.'

Wouldn't it be so much easier to step gracefully away from the computer and find something more fun to do instead? Couldn't you contribute to the world just as valuably without having to write? After all, you make a mean lemon tart – people appreciate that… As you might have guessed, these are the arguments that I say to myself on a daily basis.

However good the equivalent of your lemon tart is, I would argue that it will never replace the value of writing for you because as you said yourself, you would have let something that is important to you go. You recognise that it would be a loss not to write. I don't mean a loss for other people (although I'm sure that's true) I mean for yourself. You would not be appreciating yourself fully or acknowledging your particular ability. As the American saying goes, you wouldn't be 'your best self'.

When I mentioned my ambivalence about creative writing to my colleague Lorna, she acknowledged the contribution that my lemon tart makes but also wanted to get to the heart of the problem, and thereby find a solution. I identified that writing 'for myself' is difficult because I am quickly stalled by my inner critic, telling me how boring/rubbish/derivative etc, etc I am. I realised, however, that writing for someone else, for example, when I am ghost-writing a book or even replying to an email, it's so much easier and the words flow effortlessly.

Lorna came up with the great idea of helping me kick-start my own creative writing by tapping into this revelation. Because I find emailing pleasurable, she sends me an email on the theme of my story idea, and I reply to it. No pressure, no angst, just a simple response to her question. This has helped me because I no longer feel dwarfed by the enormity of the task. It's also made me less isolated and helped me drown out the inner critic. Another thing I noticed was that getting a fresh perspective and some oxygen into the story has inspired me. I came up with an idea for a sub-plot last night when previously my mind remained stubbornly closed to the subject.

When looking at the emotions associated with writing, it's important to remember too, that although it feels unpleasant at the time, it does reap dividends. Writing is a way of processing your thoughts and crystallising your point of view. As Will Self said:

'Fiction is my way of thinking about and relating to the world; if I don't write I'm not engaged in any praxis, and lose all purchase.'

A second benefit is that you feel a sense of pride that you have created something. You didn't shy away from it, you soldiered on and achieved. Perhaps one way to approach it is to think that there are hundreds of tasks that you dislike doing but still do, because the outcome makes it worth it, such as exercising. Exhausting, repetitive, tedious, yes, it's all these, but the sense of achievement and the rush of endorphins afterwards makes it worth it. The key is to focus on the end rather than the arduous road towards it. As writer Frank Norris said:

'Don't like to write. Like having written.'

As well as remembering the goal, it could also help to learn that it is possible to change your perspective about the process. I've been reading a lot about brain-training recently and it's made me boggle about how the brain is far more plastic than we knew. We generally believe that our feelings about things are fairly static. We think that their foundations were laid down years ago and are non-negotiable. Now, neuroscientists have discovered that these foundations are malleable. For example, in your case, you have the thought process: 'Writing makes me unhappy, therefore I don't want to do it.' This has developed because your brain has formed a neural pathway between the concept of writing and the emotion of unhappiness. The two have become linked (probably due to a negative early experience of it) so whenever you think about writing you feel down. The great news is that you can reroute your brain so it forms a new neural pathway, this time between writing and satisfaction, even happiness. The secret to this is to go outside your comfort zone and approach writing differently. Try a writing exercise that is easy and fun for just two minutes. Reward yourself afterwards. Rinse and repeat. These techniques will help carve a new pathway in your brain and you will discover that writing is not the grind you anticipate.

In conclusion, Emma, the fact that you have written to me for help suggests that you want to find a way around this problem, rather than abandoning your writing altogether, and this means that there is hope for the future. Take a deep breath, pick up your pen and start writing once more.

Try this

- » Try Lorna's strategy and start emailing a friend. Use this tactic to develop characters, plots and vignettes. The joy of the new arrival in your inbox will help you stay motivated.

- » Give your brain-training a nudge by looking back over work you feel proud of. The sense of achievement will help forge positive associations for your writing.

- » Add writing to your daily routine: Brush teeth, empty the dishwasher, write for 20 minutes. It will soon become something you do unthinkingly, rather than agonise over and berate yourself for not doing.

Notes

Twenty one
I CAN'T FINISH A STORY

Vicky, BRISTOL

There are a whole host of reasons why manuscripts remain unfinished, Vicky; boredom, becoming distracted and feeling uninspired are just three, but the fact that you actually feel sick when you think about completing one of your stories gives me a clue as to the problem. To have a physical reaction of nausea means that you associate it with fear; there is an emotional trigger when you approach an ending. What we need to do is to mine down to the heart of the matter and who better to help us but Truman Capote?

Capote referred to finishing a book as: 'just like you took a child out in the back yard and shot it' – emotions are running deep there, Truman. The idea that a work-in-progress manuscript is like a child: vulnerable, innocent, full of potential, and that completing it is the equivalent to killing it, is a potent one. Is it because when something is finished it becomes static, no longer malleable or receptive to change or improvement?

Is a writer murdering an idea by finishing a book?

Death is the ultimate ending, after all. Does this chime with you, Vicky? That wrapping-up the story, revealing how the plot is resolved, is too final? Ask yourself if this is what it could be.

Truman Capote, as well as 'giving good quote', also knew exactly what you meant. He encountered your problem whilst writing *Answered Prayers*, a book that he got a publishing deal for in 1966, just before his smash-hit *In Cold Blood* came out, but he never completed the book. In 1971, five years after he'd signed the contract (and three years after his deadline), he said on a TV chat show: 'Either I'm going to kill it, or it's going to kill me,' and referred to it as his 'posthumous novel'.

Capote's struggle illustrates just how hard it is to *write*, let alone finish anything. For some people, putting pen to paper is a momentous task, as it's very emotionally charged. You are offering yourself up to be scrutinised. The book that 'everyone's got in them' is finally landing on the page and it can be a crushing disappointment if it's not as good as you hoped. As Erica Jong admitted:

126

'I went for years not finishing anything. Because, of course, when you finish something you can be judged.'

This brings a second spike of anxiety to the mix – as well as Capote's fear of it not being *truly* finished, there's Jong's terror of other people's negativity, of not being good enough. Do your stories remain half-formed to avoid both these nasties? If this is the case, then I think now is the time to put yourself in therapy. I don't mean literally take yourself off to a counsellor, but use the same principles as a psychologist to untangle your writerly problem.

The first milestone in the therapeutic process is to acknowledge the problem, and you have already reached that one, as you know what's wrong. The next step is to understand why this is happening, and together we can crack this. Thinking deeply about the source of the queasiness – fear of failure, or of commitment (in the sense that by finishing a story you are committing to it as a completed work) are two hot chestnuts to consider. The final step is to process these emotions, to give them oxygen by bringing them out into the fresh air so you can study the fiendish things. This is a slippery thing to do (and why therapists are kept busy), but it is possible to do it on your own with some introspection.

Once you are familiar with what has been preventing you from typing 'The End' then you can start to normalise it, which in turn changes it from a demon to a challenge. Write down all the emotions that emerge when you think

of finishing a story as this will help you focus. Then when you start a new story, you can recognise when that old sicky-feeling arises, give it a name, and carry on regardless, saying, 'Hello, sicky-feeling, you're not going to stop me, this time.'

For people suffering from depression, the advice is to exercise, eat healthily and avoid alcohol, in other words, try to encourage their mood to lift by acting positively. I prescribe the literary equivalent. As hard as it undoubtedly is, where the depressive is advised to go for a walk instead of hiding under the bedclothes, I suggest you do the same – do exactly what you don't feel like doing and open up that folder of doom. Revisit your favourite unfinished story and before you have a chance to twiddle with a paperclip, write one sentence that summarises the ending. Work backwards from that sentence until it meets the point where you left off.

Whilst you're rooting around in that dreaded folder, why not follow Anton Chekhov's advice:

'My own experience is that once a story has been written, one has to cross out the beginning and the end. It is there that we authors do most of our lying.'

The fact that your stories do not have endings could be turned into a positive. Perhaps your stories do not need to be resolved, as they could either stand on their own as an interesting vignette or be amalgamated into a longer piece of writing? You could take a really experimental view and see your work as deliberately incomplete. Russian author Nikolai Gogol's unfinished work *Dead Souls* ended mid-sentence, and literary academics still debate whether this was intentional.

That folder doesn't have to be a repository of failures, because within it lies the opportunity to challenge your demons and move on. Instead of lacking endings, your stories can be just the beginning.

Try this

» The bestselling writer Dorothy Koomson once said to me that when she gets stuck writing a section, she simply starts writing a new one. This is similar to your strategy, yet what differs is that Dorothy's tactic is about the same book. In other words, don't abandon your work altogether, just take a break from one particular passage when the nausea begins to rise.

» Write an extensive outline of your story before you begin, so completing it is a matter of joining the dots rather than waiting for the muse to strike and falling prey to anxiety.

» Start with the ending so once that hurdle is overcome, writing the rest is less fraught.

Notes

Twenty two
I CAN'T COPE WITH CRITICISM

"I have been a creative writer for quite a few years now, but the emotional pain and heartache I feel whenever someone finds fault with my work still cuts me to the quick. I can't help but take it as a personal insult and I am desperately hurt and offended. How can I become more robust in the face of criticism?"

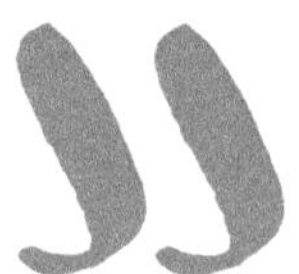

Frances, BATH

Your letter reminded me of one of the characters in *The Bone Clocks* by David Mitchell, the much fêted novelist Crispin Hershey, who is so incensed and infuriated when his long-awaited second novel is roundly trounced by a literary critic that he fumes and seethes and plots his revenge and the consequences of this follow him to the grave. Now, whilst I'm not suggesting that you take his lead, I can understand how deeply you feel about your work. It's natural to feel protective about it. Offering it up to the world is taking a risk, and you feel vulnerable and exposed as a result.

The easiest solution would be to avoid showing your work to anyone, but I imagine that part of the pleasure you gain from writing is the anticipation of praise and admiration you receive when someone reads and enjoys it. The urge to write is often coupled with the urge to share this creativity. So instead of hiding it away, you're going to have to arm yourself with some coping strategies to deal with what you perceive is negative feedback.

One tactic is to ignore it. The writer AL Kennedy, in a piece called: 'Why I don't read my reviews' says: '"I don't read reviews" does sound as if I'm happily tucked away in my own colon – but book reviews are odd things. They emerge months, if not years after the book is done with, so they're not that much use to the author. If the book's a car crash, it's already happened and we've walked or crawled away long ago.'

This is perhaps easier for published writers, but for most of us, the feedback is immediate and face-to-face. Which brings us to the next key point – you need to distinguish between constructive and destructive criticism and also evaluate the motives of the critic.

Constructive criticism is an invaluable part of a writer's toolkit. Working with an editor, who necessarily provides insights and guidance to help perfect the book, is a crucial stage in any creative endeavour. They are there to help you improve and any advice should be received with open arms. Instead of interpreting it as a judgment of your ability, see it as a gift. On the Absolute Beginners writing course that I run, feedback is one of the key benefits. As one participant said:

'Receiving feedback on my work has helped motivate me and taught me how I could improve my writing.'

It would be practically impossible to produce a polished final draft without the assistance of a second pair of eyes. At Appledore Book Festival, writer Virginia Baily spoke of her delight on finishing her novel *Early One Morning* and sending it off to her literary agent, only to be told that she had completely evaded the central story that was begging to be told. She had to admit that she had neglected to write it because it was too challenging, but ultimately she chose to face her demons and rewrite the whole book. In the end the book was all the better for it and was optioned and published by Virago.

So, after the red mist has faded slightly, try to consider whether the feedback and criticisms are valid. Would these suggestions enhance your work? Swallow your pride and try incorporating them into a second draft. You may be surprised. They may make the difference between a good story and a great story. And this process will help you accept future feedback and even welcome it. If you're not willing to listen to any criticism, then you have to accept that your work won't progress.

That's easier said than done, you may say – because it hurts. Fair enough, because the reason criticism hits so hard is because it echoes our own worst enemy: ourselves. However confident you are of your writing, there will always be a voice in your head that says: 'I knew it. I'm rubbish.' This inner critic feasts on other people's negative opinions. It seizes upon them to validate itself. But actually, you need to drown out the inner critic. Every time it crows: *You're a failure*, answer back: *I'm a success.*

On the other hand, if the motives behind the criticism aren't entirely noble, now is the time to reject it. People who give destructive criticism want to incapacitate you as a writer. This may be for a variety of reasons: anger, envy or even fear. Perhaps your efforts make them feel inadequate or intimidated? Put their negativity to one side. You have to say to yourself: *This is their stuff. This is not my problem.* Don't let them win.

I advise continuing to write, continuing to show your work to others and praising yourself for having the nerve to do it. Just as there is truth in the old adage that you can't please all of the people all of the time, it is just as likely that whilst some readers may choose to critique your work, others may respond that it has saved their life (marriage, sanity...) or at the very least, that they really enjoyed it. All you can do is write courageously from the heart and accept the praise and the criticism with equanimity.

Try this

- Go to a writing group. Reading out your work in a supportive environment will help you accept constructive criticism. You will also learn new coping strategies from others' reactions when you make suggestions about their work.

- Remember that it is not *you* the person is critiquing, but your *work*. Try to see your writing as separate to you; something that has a life of its own and that can be improved and polished.

- Choose a friend who you know is 'bookish' to appraise your work. Rather than asking: 'Did you like it?' ask leading questions such as: 'Could you think of a way to make the ending stronger?' or 'was that character convincing? Did her dialogue ring true?' Encourage them to help you tackle problem areas in your work. If you make this a regular thing, they could also help with giving you a nudge when the creative well has run dry. You never know, it may encourage them with their writing too – and you can mentor each other.

Notes

Twenty three
HOW LONG SHOULD I SPEND ON MY SECOND DRAFT?

In answer to your question, may I ask another? How long is a piece of string? A book is not finished until it is finished and unfortunately there are no short cuts. I know your frustration; the end is in sight and you're champing at the bit, but the editing process is so slow and meticulous that it can be frustrating. It would be lovely if the moment you had written the last word, you could just press 'print', pop it in the post box and wait for your acceptance letter, but unfortunately writing a book just isn't like that.

Working on a second draft of your work is the time when you really pin down exactly what you want to say, and gauge whether you have done this effectively. After the adrenalin and glamour of writing in full flow is over, the pace of editing can seem pedestrian, but must never be neglected. Ernest Hemingway managed to write an impressive 47 potential last lines for his book *A Farewell to Arms* before deciding on one he was happy with. One of his rejected attempts was: 'That is all there is to the story. Catherine died and you will die and I will die and that is all I can promise you.' Compare this to the actual ending: 'It was like saying goodbye to a statue. After a while I went out and left the hospital and walked back to the hotel in the rain.' Isn't the second one so much more effective? The first one feels perfunctory and even slightly irritable – like he was in a rush to finish the book, whilst the second one is simple, elegant and poignant. (Apologies for the spoiler if you haven't read the book!) So, boring though it may be, the second draft (or third, fourth or 47th...) is the time where some of your best writing will emerge.

My colleague, Lorna Howarth, likens it to creating a sculpture:

'Imagine you have a huge block of marble. Your first draft is the equivalent to carefully drawing the outline on it and knocking off the first chunks. The second draft is the chance to make your work shine – you chip, chip, chip away at it until it's honed to perfection.'

This is an absolutely essential part of the procedure and demands focus and an eye for detail. A book being published from the first draft is as rare as hen's teeth. Iteration, or the act of repeating a process, allows for more insight and clarity on your work, so try not to view it negatively. As Stephen King said: 'When you write a book, you spend day after day scanning and identifying the trees. When you're done, you have to step back and look at the forest.'

Lorna also makes the important point that a fresh perspective is key to a good second draft. This can be accomplished in two ways – either by yourself or with the help of others. The first can be better achieved if you step away from your work for a week or so. This gives you a chance to percolate your thoughts about it and also helps you forget exactly what you've written so you can approach it again with new eyes. The problem with attempting a second draft on your own is that you can end up going round in circles and you can often lose the original impetus of the book due to overwriting.

The second suggestion, and the one that Lorna highly recommends, is to give it to someone else to read. This could be a specialist, such as an editor who will assess the piece as a whole, or a trusted friend, preferably one who is an avid reader and whose opinion you respect. Lorna explains: 'Many people consider writing to be a solitary activity – done alone in your shed – but that's not what happens in the publishing world. The book that finally rests on your shelf is the product of a collaboration between a number of people – the writer, of course, but the editor, sub-editor, proofreader and designer all play a pivotal role.'

As well as understanding the importance of the process, gaining insight into the emotions that have been churned up is key too. Working on a second draft requires nerves of steel. It's a jittery business, pouring out your creativity for the enjoyment of others, and having to scrutinise your efforts (or having others scrutinise them) is nerve-wracking. This can explain your desire to crack on, rather than dawdle around editing, and twinned with this anxiety is impatience. It feels like your book is being delayed, but you could also interpret it as your book is well on its way to completion. Allow yourself to sit with the feeling of impatience and adopt a mindful perspective on it – 'I understand why I'm feeling this, and this feeling will pass'. Also take comfort from the words of comedian and actor Amy Poehler who identifies with your problem: 'Most authors liken the struggle of writing to something mighty and macho, like wrestling a bear. Writing a book is nothing like that. It is a small, slow crawl to the finish line. Honestly, I have moments when I don't even care if anyone reads this book. I just want to finish it.'

Good luck with your second draft, Eve, it may not be as exhilarating as writing the first, but the satisfaction when you have produced something you are proud of will be worth the wait.

Try this

» Everything in life is a series of learning curves. You can't expect to be right first time when you try something new, and your first draft is just this. Send it out to some 'beta-readers' (non-professional bookworms) and ask for their feedback, then incorporate this as you see fit in your second draft.

» Be ready for your public. You wouldn't go on stage in your under-wear (I assume); you'd take the trouble to dress up in your finery, so imagine the editing process as preparing your book for an equally exciting debut.

» For encouragement, remember the words of Vladimir Nabokov: "I have rewritten — often several times — every word I have ever published. My pencils outlast their erasers."

Notes

Twenty four
MAINTAINING MOMENTUM

I can completely understand and identify with your problem, Janine, because I too find it hard to fit creative writing around my other commitments, but what I noticed immediately about your letter is that you have one huge thing in your favour, and this is that you're keen. Enthusiasm about a hobby or project is key, otherwise what is the purpose? Writers write because they feel the need to tell their story and you can use this urge to spur you on.

Unfortunately, the received wisdom about writing is that it needs to be done regularly, so instead of working in fits and starts, try to winkle out any spare moments you have in the day that you may not have considered as writing time. This will create some sense of continuity. Kurt Vonnegut reportedly wrote for two and a half hours before breakfast – as if food was only allowed as a reward after industry. When do you think you could find time? That's easier said than done, I hear you say. Finding the time to write is a challenge in an already full schedule, but *making* the time is a different matter.

Author of the bestselling novel *Before I Go to Sleep*, S J Watson, was an audiologist and wrote his book during evenings and week-ends – proving that it's always possible to write, however busy you are. So, examine your daily routine and ask yourself what you could replace with writing. Do you really need to watch an hour of television every night? Could half your lunch hour be put aside? The secret to regular writing is that it does not have to take long. You may think that you need to set aside a chunky amount of time to write to make it worthwhile, but this needn't necessarily be the case. It is the regularity of writing – or even thinking about writing – that is important: try and do a little bit, every day.

So, instead of viewing your writing as some-thing you do 'as and when', try to bring it into everyday life. Get into the mindset of a writer by carrying a notebook around with you – or your phone, if you're technologically inclined. Whenever a thought occurs to you, jot it down, that way, you have something to refer you when you finally have a moment to sit down and focus on your work. This keeps you mentally prepared and your creative writing remains in the forefront of your mind.

You could also up the ante by giving yourself a daily target, say 500 words, to help keep disciplined. I'm a big lover of 'To-do' lists (first item on the list: write a list) – there is nothing more satisfying than being able to tick it off after you've completed your task, and at the end of the week, look back and congratulate yourself on your diligence and dedication.

Another way to maintain momentum is to add an element of fear. Fear? Yes, Janine, fear. Not fear for your life, but fear of being found lacking. The way you do this is by introducing another person into the process, such as a friend who also enjoys writing. They serve to shine the spotlight of scrutiny over your work. If there is someone else who knows what your daily or weekly word count should be then the thought of them raising a disappointed eyebrow if you haven't managed it can be enough to spur you on. You can be his/her moral gatekeeper too – it can be mutually beneficial. You could even have rewards or punishments if targets are met or missed. A friend and I set each other the challenge of writing a short story in a month. If we achieved it, we were rewarded by the other making the elaborate pudding of our choice. If we failed, we had to sing at a karaoke night at the local pub (you need to visit this pub to know what a terrifying prospect this would be). Moving writing into a social zone also helps to keep momentum by having a ready-made audience – you can look forward to sharing your work and writing for someone else gives you a reason to write.

I do understand that sometimes life gets in the way, despite your best intentions. If there has been an unavoidable lull and you're struggling to pick up the threads of your story, you can overcome this by always ensuring that you end at a point where you know exactly what's going to happen next. Don't use the fact that you've ground to a halt as a natural pause, otherwise you'll just feel disinclined to resume writing. Jeanette Winterson says:

'Never stop when you are stuck. You may not be able to solve the problem, but turn aside and write something else. Do not stop altogether.'

On a very practical level, it's also a very good idea to have a clear structure in mind, with a beginning, middle and end, so you know exactly where you're going and at what point you are at between each writing session.

Maintaining momentum is always going to be a challenge with a busy life, but the wonderful sense of accomplishment at the end of a completed piece is reward enough.

Try this

» A writing tip to get up to speed after a gap is to retype the last page of your work – it reminds you where you are and gets you back up to speed. The tapping of the keyboard also gives your brain a nudge about the creative process.

» Alternatively, you can try deleting the last page and rewriting it from memory – you may discover that it's better this time around.

» View each time you write as a slice of a bread – you are gradually building up a whole loaf, piece by piece, and it's a process that needn't be rushed.

Notes

Twenty five
I'M TOO SHY TO PUBLICISE MY BOOK

"I'm hoping to get my book published and
am aware that as a previously unpublished
author, the majority of the publicity and
marketing will be down to me. This thought
fills me with horror. I am by nature quite
reserved, indeed, one of the joys of writing
is that it is a solitary pursuit. How can
I prevent my shyness sabotaging my book's
chances of success?"

Simon, CARLISLE

Firstly, congratulations for completing a novel; that's a fantastic achievement and for many, a hurdle they are yet to conquer. In an ideal world, you would now relax and let your work speak for itself, but you're right in thinking that for your book to be successful in terms of sales, a strategic marketing and promotion plan is essential.

I can understand your reticence about self-promotion. There are several negative emotions attached to it: the fear of being pushy or making a fool of yourself, for example – but there are ways to approach book promotion without sacrificing your dignity, which we will examine shortly. But before this, I want to say that shyness need not be an affliction. Susan Cain, who wrote *Quiet: The Power of Introverts in a World that Can't Stop Talking* recognises that: everyone shines, given the right lighting.

Everyone shines, given the right lighting.

For some, it's a spotlight, for others, a lamp-lit desk. The key to success, in your case, is to find ways of approaching marketing and publicity that suits your personality.

Happily, one of the first steps in promotion you will not find too daunting, is to draw on your own contacts. Most publishers these days like to work closely with the author regarding the cover and format because they have useful connections. For example, I worked on a book recently called *The First English Explorer*, a fascinating true historical adventure. The author, Kit Mayers, was himself an explorer and had met the famous and influential Sir Ranulph Fiennes on several occasions. He was able to get a fantastic endorsement or 'puff' as it's called in the trade, for the back cover. That kind of 'contact' helps sales immensely.

So, think laterally about your own book: who do you know that might give you a sparkling puff? You may think you don't know an expert or anyone famous – but we're all experts in one way or another: who better to review a book on reducing stress at work than your friend who owns a small business? Even if they're not exactly famous, a well-written endorsement is very useful, and you may be able to put an MBA or, Creative Director after their name, which adds kudos.

If even approaching friends makes you feel like you are 'blowing your own trumpet' then it's time to take a step back and separate yourself from your work. At the root of shyness lies the fear of exposure, but it's your writing that's on show, not you. You wrote your book for a reason, a desire to tell a story that resonates with the reader. Take the attention off yourself by focusing on this. Write down the reasons why you wrote your book. Hopefully, you feel passionately about your work, so let this passion show – it's infectious.

The idea of being enthusiastic about your book may be toe-curling, but one way to steel yourself is to try the 'act as if' exercise. When you are facing something you dread, such as making a phone call, think of the most self-assured person you know, and adopt their mannerisms, posture and tone of voice. Your nerves will melt away – and if they don't, just 'act as if' they have. Eventually, you trick your mind into believing it, if only for the length of the call. A study at The University of Singapore found that clenching your fist, mimicking the gesture of determination, will help you maintain motivation and resolve, showing that simple physical actions can affect how you feel.

On a practical note, one great thing to your advantage is how promoting your book has moved on this century. The vast majority of it can be done online. You can get busy networking, publicising and marketing, all without uttering a word. As author and introvert Bob Tarte says:

'For me the introvert-extrovert thing doesn't apply a whole lot to online activity. What's more introverted than sitting alone in a room and typing with the shades down?'

You can be as gregarious as you like, when you're safely typing it on a computer screen.

So spread your net wide and start firing off emails. For ideas on who to approach, have a think about your book. For example, if you've written about health tips for children, make a list of all the people and organisations you think may be interested in it: your friends and family (never underestimate the support they will give you); your pre-school club; your regional newspaper; local radio; the local health-food shop; health and wellbeing magazines – and don't forget online forums such as mumsnet.com. Send the most hopeful contacts a pre-publication review copy which your publisher should provide you, or if you're self-publishing, you can print a short digital run first – and ask if they will review your book, give you an endorsement, stock it in their shop or club or feature it in their paper or radio show.

If you don't want to actually be interviewed, you can send newspapers and magazines a pre-prepared interview – sometimes, they will even print it verbatim. Don't forget to send a high quality jpg of the book cover, and if you can bear it, one of yourself too. People love people, and it will make all the difference if you can steal yourself for a professional-ly-taken photo.

You should also take advantage of social networking sites, but avoid simply creating a Facebook page about your book and listing all the good things about it, as people will soon get bored. If it's a novel, let the characters themselves speak about the book; you can cut and paste some juicy paragraphs of your book to entice people to want to read more; you can link to people and places that are featured in the book – so if, for example, your novel is set on the windswept coast of Blackpool, do some research – link with hotels and cafes there, and ask them to stock your book. It's worth remembering that you can tweet out the first 147 characters of any Facebook post on Twitter, so include your hashtags and handles right at the beginning.

Blogging about your book is equally important and can be very rewarding – an immediate way of connecting with the world whilst remaining in perfect solitude. Why not include a haiku a day, written by the main character in your novel? Remember to interchange your blogs and posts, so that whatever you write can be used several times in different formats.

I hope these ideas have reassured you that your personality need never be a hindrance, Simon. If you're ever in need of fortification in the months to come, remember the words of Gandhi: 'In a gentle way, you can shake the world.'

Try this

- » Solitude is a catalyst for creation. Shut the door and open your laptop.

- » Your book is your creation, so as the parent of this creation, put your feelings to one side and give it the support and encouragement you would your children.

- » If you don't like the aggressive approach of some marketing tools, such as press releases, write one in your own style: understated, interesting, unique.

Notes